HERAUSGEB

Nancy H. Kleinbaum

Dead Poets Society

with additional texts
for study at school

Erläutert von
Hans-Georg Krapf

ASCHENDORFF · MÜNSTER

Diesen Erläuterungen und allen Seitenangaben (= Randziffern) liegen die folgenden ungekürzten englischen Ausgaben zugrunde:
Nancy H. Kleinbaum: Dead Poets Society

Taschenbuch aus der ELT-Serie, Nr. 42 – 1995
ISBN 3-88389-042-1

identisch mit
der Ausgabe der Bantam Books – 1989
ISBN 0-553-28298-0

und
der Ausgabe der Petersen
Classics Bd. 170 – 2002
ISBN 3-88389-170-3

5. Auflage

Nach der neuen deutschen Rechtschreibung

Gesamtherstellung: Druckhaus Aschendorff, Münster, 2006

ISBN 3-402-02869-7

Table of Contents

A Word to the Reader

Certainly you know the movie *Dead Poets Society (Der Club der toten Dichter)*. You will remember the students in the Honor Room, huddled in a circle, and Robin Williams alias Mr. Keating whispering his magical *Carpe Diem* into their puzzled ears. Or the Dead Poets running through the frozen winter forest, their hoods over their heads. Or Neil Perry standing in his bedroom window after his father had made him come home with him. And perhaps you will also remember some lines from the poems you could hear in the movie.

Our book is supposed to help you find your way through the novelization of the script to that film.

You will find the most important vocabulary. Perhaps you will have to look up more words, but there will be enough in the wordlist to make you feel safe already.

Then you will find several of the poems, this time in their complete versions, and you will find some of the quotations in their context.

Afterwards we want to introduce you to the American school system, in general and specifically; very specifically, when we present you with recent materials from the school where the movie was made.

And finally there will be a variety of texts: about great teachers, a free electric band, and eventually about the movie itself.

You will find questions under all the texts, but we have tried to keep them quite open so that your study will not be forced too strongly into one direction. To study the details, you will certainly be able to formulate your own questions and find your own answers so that this book will be part of your own work in the end.

We hope our selection will make the reading easier for you and supply you with a background to appreciate the book (and the movie) more fully.

Select Bibliography

Brandenburg, André, *N.H. Kleinbaum: Der Club der toten Dichter, Anregungen für produktionsorientiertes Lesen*. Hollfeld, 2002[3]

Decke-Cornhill, Helene, „Interventionen: Aufforderung zum Sturm auf Bilder, Filme und andere Texte", *Der fremdsprachliche Unterricht* 1/1996, 43–47

Dirks, Una, „Mit Metaphern deuten lernen. Eine Unterrichtsreihe am Beispiel des Films *Dead Poets Society*", *Praxis des neusprachlichen Unterrichts* 2/1994, 138–151

Grindhammer, Lucille, "Hollywood in the English Language Classroom: *The Dead Poets Society*", *Neusprachliche Mitteilungen aus Wissenschaft und Praxis* 4/1993, 244–250

Krüger-Kahoula, Angelika, "Recycling Dead Poets: An English Unit For the Upper Grades", *Der Fremdsprachliche Unterricht* 4/1992, 42–46

Liebelt, Wolf (ed.), „Der Film *Dead Poets Society* im Englischunterricht: Arbeitshilfen, Filmkritiken, Aufsätze", *Materialien zur Medienpädagogik 6* (Veröffentlichungen der niedersächsischen Landesmedienstelle), Hannover, 1995

Liebelt, Wolf, „Der Film *Dead Poets Society* im Englischunterricht", *Praxis des neusprachlichen Unterrichts* 4/1996, 364–371

Vocabulary

Producing a word list for a text is always a question of selection. On the one hand all the important words should be included. On the other hand, if the word list is too long the readers will become tired of looking the words up and they will lose the joy of reading this book. And many words are known to the readers even though they have never heard them in English – be it that there are similar or identical ones in the readers' mother tongue, be it that the meaning can be derived from a word the readers are already familiar with, or be it that their context explains them. So in order to keep the size of our word list down we have concentrated on those words not listed in groups 1 to 3 of Alfred Haase's *Englisches Arbeitswörterbuch* (Frankfurt, 1975), and those not generally used in the Englishbooks for grades 5 to 10.

The pronunciation follows the 14th edition of the *English Pronouncing Dictionary* by Daniel Jones (London, 1984). It should be mentioned that we list the British pronunciation as long as the only difference to the American one is the final '-r'.

These are the abbreviations we use:
American **E**nglish/ **B**ritish **E**nglish
adjective, **adv**erb, **n**oun, **pl**ural
informal, **sl**ang
some**b**ody, some**th**ing, **o**ne**'s**, **o**neself
jeman**d**, jeman**des**, jeman**dem**

1	academy [-'---]		
	nestled ['nesld]	settled	eingeschmiegt, -gebettet
	remote [-'-]	far from everything	entlegen, fern
	Vermont [-'-]	state in the northeast of the USA	
	aisle [aɪl]	passageway, corridor e. g. in a church, plane	(Mittel-)Gang
	reverberation	echo	Echo, Widerhall
	bagpipe	musical instrument often connected with Scotland	Dudelsack
	elderly	approaching old age	älter
	swathed [sweɪðd]	wrapped in layers of cloth	eingehüllt
	robes (pl)	official garment	Robe, Umhang
	alumnus, -i; -a, -ae (AE) [ə'lʌmnəs, -aɪ; -ə, -i:]	former student	Ehemalige(r)
	slate	thin grey stone used for covering roofs	Schiefer
	hallway	spacious corridor	Eingangshalle
	venerable ['---]	demanding respect for its age	altehrwürdig
	solemnly (adv) ['sɒləmlɪ]	seriously and full of emotion	feierlich

	dais ['deɪɪs]	raised platform for a speaker	Rednertribüne, Podium
	husky	quite big and strong	stämmig, gedrungen
	to conclude	to come to an end	enden
2	audience	all the people watching an event	Zuschauer/-hörer
	excellence	the highest quality	Höchstleistung
	unlit	not burning	nicht angezündet
	to bend forward, (bent, -)	to lean forward	sich nach vorn beugen
	to pass sth	to hand over sth	etwas weiterreichen
	to intone	to speak solemnly	intonieren
	distinguished	excellent	herausragend
	to mark	to indicate	markieren
	to pause dramatically	to interrupt one's speech for effect	eine Kunstpause einlegen
	gaze	stare	starrer Blick
	intense	serious	ernst
	to bellow	to shout	laut herausstoßen
	pillar	upright piece of wood or stone to support e. g. a roof	Säule
	shuffle	sound of moving feet	Scharren
	tense	uneasy, full of tension	angespannt
3	to rise to attention, (rose, risen)	to stand still in a military position	Haltung annehmen

to hesitate	to wait before acting	zögern
to nudge sb	to push sb with o's elbow	anstoßen
drawn	tired from worrying	abgespannt
in unison ['ju:nɪzn]	sounding like one voice	im Gleichklang, einstimmig
to squeak	to make a shrill sound	quietschen
to subside [səb'saɪd]	to die down	abflauen
hush	silence	Stille
to graduate (AE)	to take finals; to be given the diploma	Examen machen; das Abgangs-zeugnis bekommen
ivy ['aɪvɪ]	plant climbing trees	Efeu
Ivy League	the 8 most prestigious universities/colleges in the NE of the USA	
effort	hard work	Bemühung, Anstrengung
to sport	to wear with pride	sich schmücken mit
curly hair	hair that is not straight	lockiges Haar
outgoing	open	offen, kontaktfreudig
build	figure	Körperbau
handsome ['hænsəm]	goodlooking	gut aussehend
preppy (infml)	smart and clean (like from an expensive prep-school)	schick und teuer

	prep (aratory) school	private school preparing for the admission to a more prestigious college or university	
	accomplishment	success after hard work	Erfolg
	Dean	head of a college or university	Dekan
	fervent	full of enthusiasm	leidenschaftlich
	dedication	devotion	Hingabe
4	to direct sb's attention toward sth	to aim sb's attention at sth	jds Aufmerksamkeit auf etwas richten
	to join the ranks of	to become a member of	sich einer Gruppe/Institution anschließen
	to rest on	to be based on	ruhen auf
	seventh grader	student aged about 12 entering secondary education	
	transfer student	student coming from another school/university	„Wechsler" von einer anderen Schule/Universität
	to squirm	to move uneasily	hin- und herrutschen, sich winden
	mention	reference	Erwähnung
	to reveal	to make visible	zeigen, verraten
	self-consciousness	uneasiness	Befangenheit, Unsicherheit

	byword	word representing an idea/institution	Inbegriff
	cornerstone (fig)	basic element in a structure	Eckpfeiler
	Welton Society, Honor Society	school societies only for the best students	
	to snap to one's feet	to jump up	aufspringen
	to beam	to smile brightly	strahlen
	smug	very pleased with o. s.	selbstgefällig
	dignity	nobility of manner or character	Würde
	fulfillment (AE; BE -fil-)	act of fulfilling	Erfüllung
5	to pat	to touch lightly	tätscheln
	encouragement	mental support	Ermutigung
	cluster	closely-packed group	Bündel, Menge
	achievement pin	pin which a pupil gets after a success	
	in a rotelike monotone ['mɒnətəʊn]	in an unvarying voice like learnt by heart	wie auswendig gelernt
	to acknowledge sth	to take notice of sth	etwas zur Kenntnis nehmen
	reward	premium	Belohnung
	due to	because of	auf Grund von
	retirement	end of work due to age	Ruhestand, Pensionierung

	beloved [bɪ'lʌvd]		
	replacement	person coming in for sb	Ersatz, Nachfolger
	graduate	person having graduated	Absolvent, „Ehemaliger“
	honors graduate	student graduating among the best of the year	
	highly regarded	very much respected	hoch geschätzt
6	faculty	all the professors of a college or university	Lehrkörper
	scholarly (adj) ['skɒləlɪ]	academic, learned	gelehrt
	to eye	to watch carefully	mustern
	class (AE)	all the students graduating in the same year	Examensjahrgang
	octogenarian [,ɒktəʊdʒɪ-'neərɪən]	person in his/her 80s	Achtzigjährige(r)
	haughtily (adv)	very proudly	hochmütig
	to shun an offer	to say no to an offer	ein Angebot ausschlagen
	painstaking	extremely careful	sehr gewissenhaft
	to mumble	to speak very unclearly	nuscheln
	barely (adv)	hardly	kaum
	to make out	to understand	verstehen
	convocation	official meeting of the members of a school or college	hier: Versammlung

	to file out	to walk out in a line	in einer Reihe hinausgehen
	chilly	quite cold	kühl
	campus grounds (pl)	location of a school/ university	Schul-/ Universitätsgelände
	weathered	damaged by the weather	verwittert
	austerity	simplicity	Kargheit
	the world beyond	the world outside	die Außenwelt
	to hug	to take sb in o's arms	umarmen
	affectionate [ə'fekʃnət]	loving	liebevoll
	to give sb a squeeze	to put o's arm around sb	den Arm um jdn legen
	landmark	characteristic sight	Wahrzeichen
	to adjust	to rearrange	ordnen, gerade rücken
7	to unearth	to dig out	ausgraben
	to chat	to make small talk	plaudern
	to pay no heed to	to pay no attention to	keine Beachtung schenken
	startled	surprised and worried	erschreckt
	name tag	label with one's name on it	Namensschild
	You have some big shoes to fill.	You must follow a great example.	Sie stehen in einem großen Schatten.

	faint	weak	schwach, leise
	to stroll	to walk slowly	schlendern
	to quiver	to tremble	zittern
	to filter out	to come out one by one	langsam und einzeln herauskommen
	to pull away	to move away	abfahren
8	raw	cold and rough	unwirtlich
	to wail	to complain loudly	klagen, jammern
	upperclassman (AE)	student in the junior or senior class	
	dorm (itory) (AE)	student residence	Wohnheim

Chapter 2

9	brogue [brəʊg]	strong regional accent	Akzent, Dialekt
	junior class	class with one year to go	Klasse 11 in USA
	staircase	corridor with stairs	Treppenhaus
	to crush one's way up	to force one's way up	sich hochdrängeln
	to dash out	to move out very fast	hinausschießen
	oak-paneled (AE; BE: -ll-)	with walls covered with oak boards	Eiche-getäfelt
	Academy Honor Room	room with the trophies and pictures of winning teams and best students	

	crinkly	full of crinkles	faltig, rissig
	to wait for one's turn	to wait after those who were first	warten, bis man an der Reihe ist
	to peer	to look curiously	starren
	second floor (AE)	floor above ground floor	erster Stock
10	intent [-'-]	full of interest	interessiert
	to spot	to detect	entdecken
	demerit (AE)	penalty point	Strafpunkt
	dour [dʊə]	strict	streng, barsch
	eagle	big bird of prey	Adler
	inner office	main room of office	Arbeitszimmer
	briefly (adv)	shortly	kurz
	awkward ['ɔ:kwəd]	not knowing what to do	unbeholfen, verlegen
11	to assign	to give individually	zuteilen
	extracurricular activities	activities outside the regular curriculum	freiwillige Schulveranstaltungen
	merit	former good work; excellence	Verdienst (fig.)
	desire	urgent wish	Verlangen
	failure to attend	not showing up at	Nichtanwesenheit bei
	required	necessary	notwendig, vorgeschrieben
	to row	to move a boat with your own power	rudern

	annual	here: yearbook	Jahrbuch
	forensics (pl; AE)	debating club on legal issues	juristischer Debattierklub
	Honor Council	school council regulating misbehaviour	Ehrenrat
	record ['--]	official list of achievements	Zeugnis
	to struggle to do sth	to try hard to do sth	sich abmühen etwas zu tun
	audible	hearable	hörbar
	bead	here: drop	Perle, Tropfen
	brow [braʊ]	forehead	Stirn
	to clench o's hands tightly	to make a tight fist	die Hände fest ballen
12	knuckle ['nʌkl]	lowest link of fingers	Knöchel
	to fight back tears	to try hard to hold back o's tears	mit den Tränen ringen
	to dismiss	to allow to leave	entlassen
	misery	unhappiness	Kummer
	to head towards	to move towards	sich auf etwas zu bewegen
	to shrug	to move o's shoulders in resignation	mit den Achseln zucken
	to groan	to make a sad noise	aufstöhnen
	grade	mark in a test/report	Schulnote
	to pull grades up	to improve marks	die Noten verbessern

	booby prize	prize for the poorest performance	Trostpreis, „Arschlochkarte“
	porter	man doing simple jobs around a building	Hausdiener
13	unclaimed	not asked for	nicht abgeholt
	to chuckle	to laugh quietly	kichern
	to fit	to be big enough for	hier: aufnehmen
	closet (AE) ['klɒzɪt]	cupboard built into the wall	Wandschrank
	to plop	to throw noisily	hinschmeißen
	a stiff (sl)	a dull or slow person	eine „Niete“
	to duck out (AE sl)	to sneak out quietly	sich verkrümeln
	jerk (AE sl)	stupid guy	Blödmann
	to show up (infml)	to appear	auftauchen
	rumo(u)r has it …	people say …	Es geht das Gerücht, …
	to ace	to get top grades in sth	in etwas ein Ass sein
	to flunk sth (AE infml)	to fail in sth	in etwas durchrasseln
	brownnosing (AE sl)	trying to get people's sympathy by every means	„Arschkriecherei“
14	to extend	to stretch out	ausstrecken
	shy	quiet and unsure of o. s.	schüchtern, scheu
	recognition	remembering you have heard/seen sth before	Wiedererkennen

	valedictorian (AE) [---'---]	student speaker at the graduation ceremony, usually the best of a class	
	National Merit Scholar	highly qualified student ranking among the best of his year nationwide	
	to nod	to move o's head in agreement	nicken
	to flatter	to say nice things to sb to get favours	schmeicheln
	trig	trigonometry	Trigonometrie
	buddy (AE infml)	pal	Kumpel
	to stammer	to speak very unclearly	stammeln

Chapter 3

15	to glare	to stare at sb like at an enemy	böse anstarren
16	raging	full of anger	zornerfüllt
	to hiss	to make a threatening sound like a snake	zischen
	to dispute sb	to questions sb's position	jds Position in Frage stellen
	lamely (adv)	without any energy	lahm
	to finish medical school (AE)	to finish o's studies of medicine	das Medizinstudium beenden
	as you please	as you like it	wie du es magst

	resolve	firm stand	Entschlossenheit
	to crumble	to fall into little pieces	bröckeln, ins Wanken geraten
	to take on	to accept a task	sich aufladen
	overwhelmed with	full of	überwältigt von
17	to tell sb off	to tell sb what one really thinks	jdm die Meinung sagen
	That's rich! (infml)	That's very amusing!	Das ist köstlich!
	to sneer	to say very ironically	spöttisch sagen
	to rip	to tear violently	reißen, „fetzen"
	to hurl	to throw with force	schleudern
	I don't let my parents walk on me!	I don't let my parents tell me what to do!	Ich lasse mich nicht von meinen Eltern herum-kommandieren!
	to be sprawled	to lie with arms and legs spread out	mit ausgestreckten Armen und Beinen liegen
	to approve loans	to allow customers to borrow money from the bank	Darlehen genehmigen
	to croak (sl)	to die	„abkratzen"
	to chuck (infml)	to give up	hinschmeißen
	cheerfully (adv)	in a good mood	gut gelaunt
	a bunch of people (infml)	a group of people	ein Haufen Leute

	to slam sth shut	to shut sth fast and noisily	etw zuknallen
	to slump onto sth	to fall heavily onto sth	sich plumpsen/ fallen lassen
18	glazed eyes	shiny eyes	schimmernde Augen
	glumly (adv)	in a depressed mood	bedrückt, niedergeschlagen
	refresher	refresher course	Auffrischungskurs
	slightly apart	a little separate	leicht abseits
	engraved	decorated	verziert
	desk set	things you need for writing on a desk	Schreibtisch-garnitur
	to plop	to drop heavily	plumpsen
	headboard	top part of a bed	Stirnbrett
	blankly (adv)	directly	direkt, unverblümt
	meek	humble and patient	sanftmütig
	to inherit	to receive sth from sb after his/her death	erben
19	Harvard	famous Ivy League university in Cambridge, MA	
	oxford cloth	special cotton cloth esp for men's shirts	Oxford-Tuch, Pikee
	to jab o's finger	to prick o's finger	sich in den Finger stechen
	to wince	to move back quickly because of pain or fear	zusammenzucken

20	class	lessons	Unterricht
	to dawn	to become brighter	dämmern
	to splash	to make wet	bespritzen
	to bald	to lose hair	kahl werden
	bespectacled	wearing glasses	bebrillt
21	assignment	task	(Haus-)Aufgabe
	sternly (adv)	strictly	streng
	project list	list of suggested tasks	Themenliste
	to be due	to have to be finished	fällig sein
	dismay [dɪsˈmeɪ]	deep sadness	Bestürzung
	fazed (AE infml)	seriously irritated	verdattert
	to drone	to talk loudly and monotonously	„leiern“
	contemporary [-ˈ---]	present-day	zeitgenössisch
	subject	theme	Thema
	to launch in	to start immediately	loslegen
	recitation	presentation of sth learnt by heart	Rezitation
	cut out for you	designed for you	für dich/euch zugeschnitten
	to ripple	to spread like little waves	sich ausbreiten
22	That guy is nuts! (sl)	That guy is crazy!	Der Kerl hat einen Knall!

	to moan	to make painful sounds	stöhnen
	to fail to do sth	not to do sth	etwas nicht tun
	to be penalized sth [i:]	to be punished with	bestraft werden mit etwas
	final grade	grade for the whole course	Gesamtnote
	to urge	to ask intensively	dringend bitten
	cosine ['kəʊsaɪn]	measurement for an angle	Kosinus
	complement	sth that completes	Komplement
	angle ['æŋgl]	corner in a geometrical figure	Winkel
	arc	curve	Bogen
	period ['pɪəriəd]	lesson	Schulstunde
	to reel off	to answer quickly	runterspulen
	staunch	firm	standhaft
	harsh	strict and loud	grob
	reprimand ['reprimɑ:nd]	official criticism	Tadel, Verweis
	to console	to comfort	trösten
	to get the pace of sth	to get the speed of sth	sich an das Tempo von etwas gewöhnen
23	to drag o. s.	to walk tiredly	sich schleppen
	to shed (-, -)	to get rid of	loswerden, abbauen
	yardstick	stick of 1 yd of length	Maßstock, „Elle“; Lineal
	to stroll	to walk casually	schlendern

	embarrassed	uneasy	verlegen
	to blush	to turn red in the face	erröten
	to stride (strode, stridden)	to walk with long steps	schreiten
	forcefully (adv)	foll of power	kraftvoll
	nimble minds	clever minds	helle Köpfe
	to gesture	to make movements to express an idea	gestikulieren
24	piercing	penetrating	durchdringend
	scholar ['skɒlə]	learned person, student	Gelehrter, Student
	Walt Whitman	famous New England poet praising the life in the growing USA (1819–92)	
	to refer to sb as	to address sb as	jdn ansprechen als
	to resume doing sth	to take up doing sth again	etwas wieder aufnehmen
	source	origin	Ursprung, Quelle
	charismatic [ˌkærɪz'mætɪk]	fascinating	fesselnd, charismatisch
	to emulate	to try to be like and as good as sb else	nacheifern
	pointer	stick to point at things	Zeigestock
	to proceed to	to go on to	weitergehen zu
	lined with	covered with	voll gehängt mit
	trophy ['trəʊfɪ]		
	of every description	of each kind	von jeglicher Art

	glass case	glass cupboard	Vitrine
	to sense	to feel	fühlen
25	roster [əʊ]	list of names and duties	Dienstplan, Anwesenheitsliste
	stanza ['stænzə]	part of a poem	Strophe
	to leaf through a text	to go through a text very quickly	durchblättern
	virgin ['vɜ:dʒɪn]	woman untouched by a man	Jungfrau
	"To the Virgins, to Make Much of Time"	poem by Robert Herrick (1591–1674)	
	to chuckle out	to laugh under your breath	vor sich hin lachen
	rosebud	unopened rose blossom	Rosenknospe
	ye (obs) [ji:]	you(r)	ihr, euer
	still	always	
	Carpe Diem (quam minimum credula postero.)	Seize the day (as you don't trust the next one at all.)	Genieße den Tag (und traue dem nächsten keinesfalls.)
	to snicker	to giggle	kichern
	lad	guy	Bursche
26	to experience	to live through	erleben
	to peruse [pə'ru:z]	to study intensively	sorgfältig prüfen
	timid	fearful, shy	ängstlich, schüchtern

	to be destined for sth ['destind]	to be chosen for sth	vom Schicksal auserwählt sein
	sober	serious	ernsthaft, nüchtern
	reflective	thoughtful	nachdenklich
	swiftly (adv)	with short fast motions	flink
	iota [aɪ'əʊtə]	Greek letter; here: tiny portion	Jota; Quentchen
	to be capable of sth	to be able to do sth	zu etwas fähig sein
	to chase	to hunt for	nachjagen
	almighty	with unlimited power	allmächtig
	deity ['di:ɪtɪ]	god/-dess	Gottheit
	to squander [ɒ]	to waste	vergeuden
	to fertilize	to support the growth of a plant chemically	düngen
	daffodil ['---]	yellow spring flower	Osterglocke
	to urge sb	to ask sb intensively	jdn drängen
	hesitant	tending to wait before acting	zögernd
27	rudely (adv)	harshly	grob
	weird [wɪəd]	odd	seltsam
	spooky	frightening	gespenstisch
	to shiver	to tremble (with cold or fear)	schaudern
	stuff (infml)	material, things	Zeug, Kram

28	to assemble	to meet	sich versammeln
	gymnasium	hall for indoor sports	Turnhalle
	required	prescribed	vorgeschrieben
	gut (infml)	fat belly	Speckbauch
	pacing	keeping up a certain speed through a run	Tempoeinteilung
	to make it through sth	to endure sth	etwas durchstehen
29	to gasp	to try to catch your breath	keuchen
	to embarrass sb to death	to make sb feel terribly ashamed	jdn zu Tode blamieren
	to monitor	to control	überwachen
	to sign out	to inform sb that you are leaving	sich abmelden
	alum (AE infml) ['æləm]	alumnus, -a	
	to pull sth (infml)	to accomplish sth with a trick	etwas tricksen
	to second sth	to support sth in an official meeting	etwas mittragen, unterstützen
	to toss	to throw carelessly	werfen, „schmeißen"
30	to change o's mind	to change o's opinion	die Meinung ändern
	perimeter [-'---]	outer edge	Begrenzungslinie
	to enclose sth	to make a line around sth	etwas einschließen

	sprawling	vast	ausgedehnt
	to flip through sth	to look through sth very quickly	etwas überfliegen
	to scribble	to write barely legibly	kritzeln
31	station wagon	car for passengers and goods	Kombi
	to mute	to silence	dämpfen, zum Verstummen bringen
	rambling	spacious	ausladend, geräumig
	mansion ['mænʃn]	big private home	Villa, „Herrenhaus"
	colonial house	big house with a porch and columns	
32	sharply dressed	dressed over-elegantly	erlesen gekleidet
	to stick out (stuck, -)	to hold out	ausstrecken
	You're the spitting image of your father. (infml)	You look just like your father.	Du bist deinem Vater wie aus dem Gesicht geschnitten.
	soda	sparkling water	Sprudel
	case	law suit	(jurist.) Fall
	GM	General Motors	US-Automobilkonzern
33	cute	nice-looking	niedlich
	plain	not impressive	unauffällig

	to strew	to spread out	verstreuen
	to glance at sb	to look at sb/sth from the corner o's eye	jdm einen Blick zuwerfen
	his eyes stayed glued [glu:d]	his eyes stayed fixed	seine Augen blieben kleben
	slender	slim	schlank
	giggle ['gɪgl]	high-pitched laugh	Kichern
	to recall sth	to call sth back into o's memory	sich etwas ins Gedächtnis zurückrufen
	to be stuck	to be unable to move or get any further	festsitzen, nicht weiterkommen
	to reminisce [,remɪ'nɪs]	to tell from one's fond memories	in Erinnerung schwelgen
	to weasel a settlement (AE infml)	to reach a secret settlement	eine Einigung ausmauscheln
	fee	money you pay for services	Honorar, Gebühr
	client ['klaɪənt]		
	son of a gun (AE sl)	rascal	Teufelskerl, Halunke
34	to roar	to speak very loudly	brüllen
	desperate	without hope	verzweifelt
	to fake	to pretend	vortäuschen
	his eyes darted to	he shot quick glances at	er warf kurze Blicke auf
	a big deal (AE infml)	a big affair	eine große Sache

	to shoot sb a smile	to smile at sb very briefly	jdm ein Lächeln zuwerfen
	wicked	full of secret ideas	verschlagen
35	bickering	aimless quarrel	Zankerei
	flatly (adv)	uninterestedly	lahm
	A Midsummer Night's Dream	drama by William Shakespeare (1564–1616)	
	to flunk out (AE infml)	to have to leave school etc. due to bad scores	abgehen müssen
36	to confide	to tell as a secret	anvertrauen
	to pound	to beat heavily	hämmern
	envy ['--]	longing for sb's property, boy-/girlfriend etc.	Neid
	to stagger	to walk clumsily	taumeln
	to assemble	to put together	zusammenbauen
	crystal radio ['krɪstl]	primitive radio	Diodenempfänger
	to progress [-'-]	to move forward	fortschreiten
	to collapse [-'-]	to break down	zusammenbrechen
	shell-shocked (fig)	totally irritated	verstört
	engaged	planning to get married	verlobt
	Mr. Mondo Jocko	Mr. Super-Sportsman	Mr. Muskel
	to go for	to be attracted by	schwärmen für
	matter-of-factly (adv)	soberly	sachlich, nüchtern

	to figure out	to calculate	berechnen
37	to be off on a tangent (AE infml)	to have lost one's course	aus der Spur geraten
	sheepishly (adv)	embarrassedly	verlegen
	to propose	to suggest getting married	einen Heiratsantrag machen
	to implore	to ask full of emotion	flehen
	to resume	to take up again	wieder aufgreifen
	chick (sl)	girl, woman	„Biene“
38	preface ['prefɪs]	introduction to a book	Vorwort
	entitled [ɪn'taɪtld]	carrying the title	betitelt
	poetry	lyrics	Lyrik
	Phd	Doctor of Philosophy	Dr. phil.
	to be fluent with sth	to know sth inside out	sich genau auskennen mit
	meter (AE; BE: metre)	system of stressed and unstressed syllables in a line	Versfuß
	rhyme [raɪm]		
	to render an objective	to present a principal idea	eine Kernidee wiedergeben
	to rate	to evaluate and rank	bewerten
	to determine	to decide about	bestimmen
	to plot	to mark	eintragen
	to yield	to have as a result	ergeben

	sonnet ['--]	poem of 14 lines with fixed rhyming patterns	Sonnet
	both … and …	as well … as …	sowohl … als auch …
	thereby	by that means	dadurch
	to reveal	to show sth hidden	offenbaren
	shading	filling up with lines	Schraffur
39	rating method	method of ranking	Bewertungs-methode
	to evaluate sth [ɪ'væljʊeɪt]	to work out the value of sth	etwas bewerten
	refuse, garbage ['refju:s]	rubbish; nonsense	Müll; Unsinn
	pus [pʌs]	yellowish liquid from infected wounds	Eiter
	to grab	to pick up quickly	schnell nach etwas greifen
	to deposit sth	to put sth down	ablegen, abliefern
	Make a clean tear!	Tear it out completely!	Reißt das sauber raus!
	to caution	to give a slight warning	warnend auf etwas hinweisen
	disgraceful	absolutely embarrassing	schändlich, ein Schandfleck
	to peek	to look cautiously	spähen
	alarmed	worried, irritated	beunruhigt
	baffled	confused	verblüfft

	to back out	to move out backwards	rückwärts rausgehen
40	to strut	to march proudly	stolzieren
	to stomp	to tramble down on sth	auf etwas herumtrampeln
	juncture	moment of decision	Nahtpunkt, Scheidepunkt
	to succumb to [sə'kʌm]	to give in to	sich unterwerfen, beugen
	vine	bush with grapes	Rebstock
	to savo(u)r	to enjoy a flavour or smell	genießen
	twerp (sl)	stupid person	„Rindvieh", „Hohlkopf"
	boil	painful infected swelling	Furunkel
	to tense	to show uneasiness	sich anspannen
	jerkily (adv)	with short, hard movements	ruckartig
	actually (adv)	really	tatsächlich
	to indicate	to suggest	andeuten
	wryly (adv)	ironically	ironisch
41	to argue	to put forward an argument	argumentieren
	ambition	goal	ehrgeiziges Ziel
	defiantly (adv) [dɪ'faɪəntlɪ]	challenging an opposition	herausfordernd
	drivel	nonsense	Gefasel
	passion	strong emotion	Leidenschaft

	to sustain [-'-]	to keep in existence	erhalten
	poetry	lyric quality of a poem	Poesie
	"O me! O life!"	from Walt Whitman, *Leaves of Grass* (1855)	
	romance [-'-]	romatic involvement	Romantik; Zauber
	to recur [rɪ'kɜ:]	to return	wiederkehren
	amid	among	inmitten
	to contribute [-'--]	to add as your share	beitragen
42	awestruck	full of respect	ehrfurchtsvoll
	all eyes were riveted on	all eyes were glued on	alle Augen klebten an
	impassioned	filled with passion	leidenschaftsvoll
	notion	idea	Vorstellung
	William Wordsworth	romantic English poet (1770–1850)	
	romanticism	romatic thought	Romantik

Chapter 6

43	frame	here: body	Gestalt
	fascinating ['fæsɪneɪtɪŋ]		
	misguided	inappropriate	deplatziert
	undeniably (adv) [ˌʌndɪ'naɪəblɪ]	certainly, truly	unbestreitbar
44	to miss the point	to misunderstand the main point	die Hauptsache nicht verstehen

	to peg sb as	to count sb among	jdn zu … zählen
	cynic	person ignoring all traditional values	Zyniker
	unfettered	freed	befreit
	lecture	professoral speech	Vorlesung
	guy (AE infml)	lad	Kerl
	to puff	to breathe quickly to catch your breath	keuchen
	engaged in animated conversation	talking intensively	in lebhafter Unterhaltung
	Cambridge-bound	heading for Cambridge	auf dem Weg nach Cambridge
	to be likely to do sth	to be expected to do sth	wahrscheinlich etwas tun
	thigh	upper part of leg	(Ober-)Schenkel
	thigh man (AE sl)	man with a strong interest in women's thighs	
	hell-raiser (AE sl)	guy full of ideas	Teufelskerl
45	caption [ˈkæpʃn]	text underneath a picture	Bildunterschrift
	to nudge	to hit sb/sth secretly with o's elbow etc	anschubsen
	Rhodes scholar	scholar holding an exclusive Oxford grant	Rhodes-Stipendiat
	research [rɪˈsɜːtʃ]	careful study for new facts	Forschung
46	to catch up with sb	to reach sb	jdn einholen

	split second	part of a second	Sekundenbruchteil
	to regain	to get back	wiedergewinnen
	composure [kəm'pəʊʒə]	mental stability	Fassung, Haltung
	to press	to insist	drängen
	favo(u)rable	positive	günstig
	to scan	to check a wide area quickly	überfliegen
	instantly (adv)	at once	sofort
	to be dedicated to	to be committed to	sich als Aufgabe setzen
	marrow	soft matter inside of bones	Knochenmark
	Henry David Thoreau ['θɔ:rəʊ]	transcendentalist New England poet (1817–62)	
	to invoke	to quote because of magic power	feierlich zitieren
	to take turns doing sth	to do sth one after the other	etwas einer nach dem anderen tun
	Percy Bysshe Shelley	romantic English poet (1792–1822)	
	enchantment [-'--]	magic spell	Verzauberung
47	bewildered [bɪ'wɪldəd]	confused	verwirrt, verwundert
	to participate	to take part in sth	teilnehmen
	to drip	to come out in drops	tropfen

	to swoon	to lose consciousness with excitement	dahinsinken, das Bewusstsein verlieren
	to soar	to rise to great heights	sich in den Himmel erheben
	pledge	sb waiting for admittance to a group	Anwärter, -in
	apprenticeship	time of learning a trade	Lehrzeit
	alas [ə'læs]	(expression of sorrow)	ach; leider!
	lowly	humble	bescheiden
	initiate [ɪ'nɪʃɪət]	novice	Novize
	stream	creek	Bach
48	to relent	to give in	einlenken
	No kidding! (infml)	Seriously!	Ernsthaft!
	to retort	to give an aggressive answer	zurückschlagen, scharf erwidern
	Who's in?	Who is taking part?	Wer ist dabei?
	to silence an argument	to stop a controversy	einen Streit schlichten
	to horse around sb	to dance around sb noisily	laut um jd herumtanzen
49	mystified	puzzled	verblüfft
	to figure	to imagine	sich vorstellen
	to summon	to call together	zusammenrufen
	study hall (AE)	room for independent work; time set for it	Lesesaal; selbständige Arbeit, Hausaufgaben

	in a hushed voice	in a low voice	mit gedämpfter Stimme
	to stammer	to speak barely understandably	stammeln
	study proctor (AE)	study supervisor	Aufsicht
	suspicious	distrustful	misstrauisch
50	out of earshot	too far to listen	außer Hörweite
	incredulous [-ʹ---]	unbelieving	ungläubig

Chapter 7

51	to talk in low tones	to talk in a low voice	leise reden
	well-worn	showing the signs of use	abgenutzt
	anthology [ænˈθɒlədʒɪ]	collection of poetry or short prose pieces	Anthologie, Sammlung
	written in longhand	written in normal hand-writing	hand-geschrieben
	inscription	short piece of writing	Eintragung, Inschrift
	signature [ʹ---]	one's name written by o. s.	Unterschrift
	to skim	to leaf through fast	durchblättern
	vaguely (adv)	unclearly	hier: schwach (fig)
	to be aware of sth	to realize sth	sich einer Sache bewusst sein
52	resident dorm marshal (AE)	teacher living in a dorm and keeping order	Hauslehrer

	gnarled maple tree [na:ld]	old maple tree covered with knobs	knorriger Ahorn
	to bundle o. s. in sth	to wrap o. s. in sth	sich in etwas einmummeln
	flashlight	electric lamp carried in the hand	Taschenlampe
	to startle	to shock	erschrecken
	to home in on sth	to move directly towards sth	auf etwas zusteuern
	eerie ['ɪərɪ]	spooky	unheimlich
	pine forest	forest of pine trees	Kiefernwald
	to trudge	to walk slowly and with heavy feet	stapfen
	brush	small trees and low bushes	Unterholz
53	to pop	to appear very quickly	hervorschießen
	to shriek	to scream in a very high voice	kreischen
	to crowd into	to cram into a small space	sich hineindrängen
	barren	unpleasant and cold	öde, trist
	sanctuary ['sænktʃʊərɪ]	holy place	Weihestätte
	to reconvene [ˌrɪ:kən'vi:n]	to call together again	wieder einberufen
	chapter (esp AE)	local branch	Ortsgruppe
	to conduct	to organize and lead	durchführen, leiten

	to keep minutes	to take notes officially in a meeting	das Protokoll führen
	deliberately (adv)	consciously	entschieden, bewusst
	to put to rout [raʊt]	to defeat totally and drive away	in die Flucht schlagen
54	confidently (adv)	not fearing failure	zuversichtlich
	blazing	burning brightly	flammend
	maid	girl, young woman	Mädchen
	infinite ['---]		
	tender	sensitive	sanft, zart
	to freeze (froze, frozen)	to become totally stiff from cold, fear	hier: erstarren
55	wit	intelligence, wisdom	Gescheitheit, Witz
	alleged [ə'ledʒd]	claimed but unproven	vorgeblich
	prowess ['praʊɪs]	bravery	Kühnheit, Können
	"We are the music makers …"	from the poem "Ode" by Arthur O'Shaugnessy	
	sea-breaker	construction breaking the power of the sea	Mole
	desolate ['desələt]	barren	trostlos
	to forsake (-sook, -saken)	to give up, leave for good	entsagen, verlassen
	to gleam	to shine	schimmern, funkeln

	deathless	immortal	unsterblich, ewig
	ditty	short, simple song/poem	Weise
	fabulous	like a fable	fabelartig, mystisch
	to fashion	to shape	formen, gestalten
	to go forth	to move forward	vortreten
56	Nineveh ['nɪnɪvə]	capital of Assyria, destroyed 612 B.C.	Ninive
	Babel	prehistoric capital of Babylonia	Babylon
	mirth	joy	Heiterkeit, Freude
	to utter	to express	sagen
	to overthrow	to destroy	umstürzen, vernichten
	"Out of the night ..."	from the poem "Invictus" by W. E. Henley	
	pit	access to a mine	Schacht
	unconquerable	undefeatable	unbesiegbar
	to scoff	to mock	spotten, höhnen
57	thee (obs)	you (obj)	dich
	Cool it! (sl)	Calm down!	Reg dich ab!
	to growl [aʊ]	to say sth in a low and threatening voice	knurren
	to huddle	to sit together very closely	sich zusammenkauern
	dim	barely lit	düster
	my purpose holds	it is my aim	Ich habe vor

	temper	character	Wesen, Charakter
	to strive (strove, striven)	to work/fight for sth	streben, kämpfen
	to yield	to give in	weichen, den Vortritt lassen
	Ulysses [ju:'lɪsɪ:z]	legendary Greek hero of the Trojan War	Odysseus
	Alfred Lord Tennyson	English poet (1809–92)	
	statement of purpose	declaration of the aims of sth	Zielbestimmung
	to pound out a rhythm	to beat a rhythm heavily	einen Rhythmus hämmern
	congo, conga	Cuban dance	Conga
58	"Fat black bucks …"	from "The Congo", poem by Vachel Lindsay (1879–1931)	
	buck (infml)	here: guy	hier: Kerl
	to sag	to sit with hanging shoulders	zusammengefallen sitzen
	to reel	to sway	schwanken, taumeln
	silk	fine, shiny cloth	Seide
	revel ['revl]	noisy feast	Feierei
	in derision	with a haughty laugh	spöttisch
	Congo	river (and former state) in Central Africa	Kongo
	to be entranced [ɪn'tra:nst]	to lose awareness of o's surroundings	betäubt, verzaubert sein

	compelling	attracting o's total attention	mitreißend
	to whoop [hu:p]	to scream with joy	herumschreien
	ridiculous [-'---]	laughable	lächerlich
	pitch-black	black as the night	pechschwarz
	to shiver	to shake with cold	zittern
59	exhilaration [ɪg,zɪlə'reɪʃn]	great joy	Begeisterung
	imagination	power of dreaming up things	Vorstellungskraft, Phantasie
	clearing	treeless area in forest	Lichtung
	twig	thin branch	Zweig
	to tiptoe	to walk on one's toes	auf Zehenspitzen gehen
	vigorous ['---]	energetic	kraftvoll
	morose [mə'rəʊs]	in a pessimistic mood	verdrießlich
	to woo sb	to try to get sb's attention	jdn umwerben
	endeavo(u)r [ɪn'devə]	effort	Unterfangen
	it will not do	it will not be enough	es wird nicht ausreichen
	quotation	word by word repetition of a text passage	Zitat
60	creed	religious faith, denomination	Glaubensrichtung

	school	philosophical group	(philosophische) Schule
	in abeyance [-'--]	without a final answer	in der Schwebe
	to permit [-'-]	to allow	erlauben
	hazard	risk	Risiko
	without check	without connection	verbindungslos
	to be conditioned	to be taught, trained	erzogen, geprägt sein
	to strip o. s. of sth	to remove sth from o. s.	sich einer Sache entledigen
	prejudice	unfair judgment without knowing all the facts	Vorurteil
	to leap	to jump	springen
	constantly (adv)	permanently	dauernd
	to force o. s./sb	to make o. s./sb do sth	sich/jdn zu etwas zwingen
	to consider	to think about	berücksichtigen
61	desperation	absolute hopelessness	Verzweiflung
	to be resigned to sth	to give in to sth	wegen etwas aufgeben
	to crash	to make a loud noice	krachen
	boisterous	noisy and cheerful	ausgelassen
	to deliver a poem	to recite a poem	ein Gedicht vortragen
	baffled	irritated	verwirrt
	impish	like a gnome in the woods	koboldhaft

	to scare sb to death	to cause terrible fear in sb	jdn zu Tode ängstigen
	mole	little black furry animal living underground	Maulwurf
	to pretend	to behave as if	so tun als ob
	lightning bolt	flash of lightning	Blitzstrahl
	hint of a smile	very short smile	Andeutung eines Lächelns
	to have time off	not to have to work for a time	Zeit frei haben
	lacrosse [-'-]	ball game slightly similar to hockey	Lacrosse
62	to cruise around	to drive aimlessly	herumfahren
	furious	full of energy	ungestüm
	to board	to enter a vehicle	einsteigen
	marching band	school brass band	Marschkapelle
	drum roll	rapid beat of drums	Trommelwirbel
	scale	standard sequence of musical notes	Tonleiter
	padded	protected with cushions	gepolstert
	to shove [ʃʌv]	to push with your shoulders	drängen
	to rush up	to run forward	vorlaufen
	gear	equipment	Ausrüstung
	to fantasize about sth	to dream of sth	sich etwas ausmalen
	embrace	hug	Umarmung

	to come up with sth	to produce/find sth	auf etwas kommen
63	pad	pile of paper	Block
	to scratch sth out	to erase sth	etwas durchstreichen
	flushed with	burning with	glühend vor
	dummy (AE sl)	(term for a stupid person)	Dummkopf
	to put on a play	to produce a play	ein Stück aufführen
	tryout ['--]	test showing of a play	Probevorstellung
	to act	to play in a drama	schauspielen
	summer stock	summer performances	Sommerrepertoir, -aufführungen
	audition	test for people wanting to act	Vorsprechen
64	to clench one's fist	to make a fist	die Faust ballen
	part	part in a play	Rolle
	as far as I'm concerned	as for me	was mich betrifft
	bull (AE sl)	short for: bullshit (i. e. nonsense)	Mist, Blödsinn
	to disobey sb	not to follow sb's orders/ wishes	nicht gehorchen
65	to grimace [grɪ'meɪs]	to make a face	ein Gesicht ziehen
	incredulous [-'---]	unbelieving	ungläubig

	to be supposed to do sth	to be meant to do sth	etwas tun sollen
	defensive	slightly offended	eingeschnappt
	stirred up	moved	aufgewühlt
	cesspool	container for liquid human/animal waste	Jauchegrube
	to appreciate [ə'prɪ:ʃɪeɪt]	to be grateful for	dankbar sein für
	to butt out (AE sl)	to stop giving unwanted advice	sich raushalten

CHAPTER 8

67	to explore	to examine closely	erkunden
	the nooks and crannies	i. e. every single spot	alle Ecken und Winkel
	to carve into	to cut into a softer material	einschnitzen
	moron (sl) ['mɔ:rɒn]	(term for a very stupid person)	Schwachkopf
68	in despair	desperately	verzweifelt
	brain	here: mastermind	hier: Superhirn
	romantic	romantic writer	Romantiker
	experimenter	person trying out things	Experimentierer
	to dabble in sth	to do sth for fun	sich aus Liebhaberei mit etwas beschäftigen
	to settle	to stop moving around	zur Ruhe kommen

	his face lit up	he became cheerful	seine Miene hellte sich auf
	hereby	by this means	hiermit
	to declare sth to be	to proclaim sth to be	etwas für … erklären
	Wait a minute!	Hold on!	Einen Moment!
	to object	to contradict, protest	widersprechen, protestieren
	to claim sth	to want to have sth	einen Anspruch auf etwas erheben
69	to counter	to hit back	kontern
	reluctant	unwilling	widerwillig
	instructor	coach	Trainer
	roll	class list	Klassenliste
70	to crumple	to press into many folds	zusammenknüllen
	capriciousness [kə'prɪʃəsnɪs]	impulsivity	Launenhaftigkeit, Unberechenbarkeit
	devotee [ˌdevəʊ'ti:]	enthusiastic follower	fanatischer Anhänger
	inherently (adv)	in its natural form	von Natur aus
	to excel [-'-]	to show o's best	sich auszeichnen
	gifted	born with many natural abilities	begabt
	contest ['--]	competition	Wettstreit
	sophist ['sɒfɪst]	enlightened Greek philosopher	Sophist, Anhänger einer aufgeklärten griechischen philosophischen Gruppe

	orator [ˈɒrətə]	speaker	Redner
	slip of paper	piece of paper	Zettel
	to line up	to stand in a line	sich hintereinander anstellen
	single file	one behind the other	einer hinter dem anderen
	listless	uninterested	lustlos
	against great odds	against superior powers	gegen große Widrigkeiten
	undaunted	fearless	unverzagt
71	to blare sth	to turn sth loud	etwas laut stellen
	strains (pl)	tune	Klänge
	to stand sth	to bear sth	etwas aushalten
	strife	struggle	Kampf
	torture	use of extreme pain	Folter
	popular odium [ˈəʊdjəm]	being hated by all	Hass des Volkes
	squarely (AE adv)	directly	direkt, ohne Schnörkel
	with great intent	determinedly	entschlossen
	determination	energy	Entschlossenheit
72	half-composed	half-completed	halb vollendet
	to grind out (ground, -)	to produce without inspiration	sich abringen
	to yell	to shout loudly	schreien
	Pipe down! (infml)	Shut up!	Halt die Klappe!

	to cheer	to shout with joy	jubeln
73	contentment [-'--]	satisfaction	Zufriedenheit
	revelation [ˌrevə'leɪʃn]	recognition of the truth	Erleuchtung
	by all means	under all circumstances	auf jeden Fall
	to conjure up sth ['kʌndʒə]	to bring up sth through magic	etwas heraufbeschwören
	salvation day	the day of rescue from o's sins	der Tag der Erlösung
	doomsday	the last day of the world	das Jüngste Gericht
	to enlighten	to show sb the truth	erleuchten, aufklären
	to thrill	to excite	erregen
	inspired	in the right spirit	vom richtigen Geist beseelt
	immortal [-'--]	never dying	unsterblich
74	to starve	to die from hunger	verhungern
	eventually (adv)	finally	am Ende, schließlich
	to volunteer [--'-]	to do sth out of one's own will	sich freiwillig melden
	agony ['---]	terrible suffering	Todesqualen
	lad (infm)	guy	Bursche
	misery	extreme unhappiness	Elend
	condemned	found guilty	verurteilt
	worthless	without value	wertlos

	stride	step	Schritt
	to sound	to make audible	erschallen lassen
	demonstration	public display	Vorführung
75	to lunge	to attack quickly	einen Ausfall machen
	fierce	wild	wild, heftig
	barbarian [-'---]	barbaric person	Barbar
	after all	finally	doch, schließlich
	gibberish	incomprehensible language	Kauderwelsch
	to flick	to appear quickly	aufblitzen
	to prompt	to help with a word	einhelfen
76	to choke	to cut off one's breathing	würgen
	to coax [kəʊks]	to persuade kindly	zureden
	defiant [dɪ'faɪənt]	full of resistance	trotzig
	cadence	rhythm of speaking	Sprechrhythmus
	an air of confidence	an expression of trust in o's abilities	ein Anflug von Zuversicht
77	battered	damaged	beschädigt, verbeult
	lampshade	top part of a lamp	Lampenschirm
	cord	string	Schnur
	stake	stick	Stab
	to illuminate	to put light on sth	beleuchten
	exposure [-'--]	openness to the influence of weather etc.	Ausgesetztsein

	to clear o's throat	to get sth out of o's throat noisily	sich räuspern
	random	chosen spontaneously	willkürlich
	blaring	shrill	schrill
78	to tumble	to move unsteadily	taumeln
	haunting	bewitching	verzaubernd
	sonorous [-'--]	having a deep, clear sound	volltönend
	mock	ironically imitated	aufgesetzt
	to wail out	to complain loudly	laut beklagen
	torment ['--]	pain	Qual
	I can't take it anymore!	I can't bear it!	Ich halte das nicht mehr aus!
79	embarrassment	feeling of shame and uneasiness	Scham
	to feel obliged	to feel one has to do sth	sich verpflichtet fühlen
	to stand by sb	to support sb	jdm zur Seite stehen
	fellow poet	here: colleague	Dichter-Kollege
	to dial a phone number	to ring a phone number	eine Nummer wählen
	to panick	to lose one's nerves	in Panik geraten
80	overcome	overwhelmed	überwältigt
	yelp	cry of joy	Freudenschrei

81	rehearsal [rɪ'hɜ:sl]	practice session for drama etc.	Probe
	brick	reddish-brown baked artificial stone	Backstein, Klinker
	rack	construction to put things in	Gestell
	director	person leading a drama-/ film-production	Regisseur
	jester	person paid to make jokes at medieval courts	Hofnarr
	prop girl	woman who hands out things used on stage	Requisiteurin
	curst (obs)	under bad magic	verflucht
82	Cupid	Roman god of love	Cupido
	knavish ['neɪvɪʃ]	full of bad ideas	schurkenhaft
	Hermia	one of the main characters in *A Midsummer Night's Dream*	
	to be in charge of	to be responsible for	verantwortlich sein für
	to take great delight in sth	to enjoy sth very much	großes Vergnügen an etwas empfinden
	weary [ɪə]	exhausted	erschöpft
	in woe	in sorrow	kummer-, sorgenvoll
	bedabbled with	moist from	feucht von

	dew	liquid on grass after cool nights	Tau
	brier ['braɪə]	wilde rose; thorny bush	Wildrose
83	to pump up	to pedal with all o's force	hinaufkeuchen
	motionless	without moving	bewegungslos
	chattering teeth	teeth moving uncontrollably	klappernde Zähne
	monogrammed ['---]	decorated with o's initials	mit den Anfangs-buchstaben verziert
	to mock	to make an ironic remark	spotten
	awkward	unpleasant, embarrassing	unangenehm
84	a big to-do (infml)	a big affair	eine ganz große Sache
	to underestimate	not to recognize the real value of sth	unterschätzen
	flippant	joking	schnippisch, spöttisch
	baseball bat	wooden club used for playing baseball	Baseballkeule
	infected by	affected, like by a disease	angesteckt von
	chemical ['kemɪkl]	chemical substance	Chemikalie
	screwed up (AE sl)	crazy	verrückt, „verkorkst“
85	anguished ['æŋgwɪʃt]	painful	gequält
	to grope	to search aimlessly	ziellos suchen

	courtyard	square with walls or buildings around	Innenhof
	to seep into	to infiltrate slowly	einsickern
86	to walk in step	to walk in the same rhythm	im Gleichschritt gehen
	cadence ['keidns]	rhythm	Rhythmus
	to emanate from	to come from	ausgehen von
	pavement	stony street surface	Pflaster
	commotion	noisy excitement	Unruhe, Tumult
	to pick up on a cadence	to walk in a faster rhythm	das Schritttempo anziehen
	to clap out a beat	to clap in a certain pattern	den Takt klatschen
	to distract	to move sb's attention away	ablenken
	drill-team	team doing a drill together	Exerziergruppe
	his eyebrows furrowed ['fʌrəʊd]	he raised his eyebrows	er hob die Augenbrauen
	to frown at sb	to look at sb with disapproval	die Stirn runzeln
	stride	way of walking	Gangart
	lurch	unsteady movement	Taumeln
	bounce	little jump	Hüpfer
	marked	clearly visible	deutlich

	to single out sb	to pick sb out of a group for special mention	jdn aussondern, hervorheben
87	to maintain	to keep up	aufrechterhalten
	need	urgent wish	Bedürfnis
	odd	strange	seltsam
	"Two roads diverged in a wood ..."	from the poem "The Road Not Taken" by Robert Frost, New England poet (1874–1963)	
	to diverge [daɪ'vɜ:dʒ]	to lead into different directions	sich gabeln
	that makes all the difference	that is the most important point	darauf kommt es an
	rooted	unable to move	angewurzelt
	to salute	to greet	(formell) grüßen
	to disperse	to split up	sich zerstreuen
	antic [-'-]	spleen	Marotte
	to grade a paper	to mark a paper	eine Arbeit korrigieren
	to pass sth along	to circulate a message	etwas weitersagen
	to sway	to move unsteadily	schwanken
	gusty wind	wind blowing strongly in sudden movements	böiger Wind
88	rustle [rʌsl]	sound of leaves and branches	Rascheln
	Isn't he precious? (infml)	Isn't he a darling?	Ist er nicht ein Schatz?

	to ooze	to say flatteringly	säuseln
89	flabbergasted at (AE infml)	very surprised about	völlig baff über
	announcement	proclamation	Ankündigung
	in keeping with	in agreement with	in Übereinstimmung mit
	to squeeze	to press	(sich) drücken
	to shoot sb a look, (shot, -)	to give sb a quick glance	jdm einen schnellen Blick zuwerfen
	to scrape off	to scratch off	abkratzen
	mud	wet soil	Schlamm
	he wiped it on his face	he covered his face with it	er wischte es über sein Gesicht
	brave	warrior	Krieger, Kämpfer
	to tramp	to walk noisily	trampeln
90	overcoat	long warm outer garment	Mantel
	to straighten a tie	to put a tie in the right place	eine Krawatte richten
	fraternity (AE)	society for male students	Studentenverbindung
	to make out (AE sl)	to be busy petting	knutschen
	oblivious to	forgetting	vergessend
	Make yourself at home!	Behave like at home!	Mach dir's gemütlich!
	dejected	sad, frustrated	niedergeschlagen
91	log	part of a tree	Baumstamm

	to object to	to be against	Einspruch erheben gegen
	to bump into sb	to run into sb	jdn anrempeln
	spontaneous [spɒn'teɪnjəs]		
	towny (infml)	person from the town	Städter
	to choke	to be unable to speak	es verschlägt jdm die Stimme
92	jerk-off (AE sl)	stupid person	Blödmann
	to seethe with anger	to boil with anger	vor Wut kochen
	to make out (AE infml)	to get along	klarkommen
	he is in for sth	sth (bad) is waiting for him	etwas (Schlechtes) steht ihm bevor
	butler's pantry	small room between kitchen and dining room	Anrichtezimmer
	line-backer	defensive player in American football	
93	bourbon [ɜː]	American whisky	Bourbon
	a tiny splash of coke	a small amount of coke	ein winziger Schuss Cola
	to click glasses with	to make one's glasses touch	mit jdm anstoßen
	to drain a glass in one swallow	to empty a glass without putting it down	ein Glas in einem Zug leeren
	to follow sb's lead	to follow sb's example	jds Beispiel folgen

	he burst into a coughing fit ['kɒfɪŋ]	he had to cough very badly	er hatte einen Hustenanfall
	What has he been up to?	What has he done?	Was hat er so getrieben?
	to hiccup	to have air coming up from o's stomach	„hicksen", den Schluckauf haben
94	to slap sb	to hit sb	jdn schlagen
	mesmerized ['mez-]	totally fascinated	gebannt
	to sputter	to burn irregularily	flackern
	pitted	covered with dents	zerbeult
	pint [paɪnt]	eighth of a gallon	etwa ½ Liter
	to sip	to drink in small portions	nippen
	to take a swig	to have a drink	einen Schluck nehmen
	he managed to keep from coughing	he was able to suppress a cough	ein Husten unterdrücken
95	to publish	to have printed	veröffentlichen
	to demand	to ask for sth urgently	fordern
	to beat off (sl)	to masturbate	„sich einen runterholen"
	proofer	person checking prints for mistakes	Korrekturleser
	to boast	to tell with too much pride	angeben
	to figure out (AE infml)	to guess	sich zusammenreimen

	to coo	to speak in a soft voice	gurren
	ass (AE sl)	buttocks	Arsch
96	"Shall I compare thee to a summer's day?"	from "Sonnet XVIII" by William Shakespeare	
	thee (obs)	you (obj)	dich
	thou (obs) [ðaʊ]	you (subj)	du
	art (obs)	are	bist/seid
	temperate	moderate	mild
	she melted into warm goo (AE sl)	she melted away	sie schmolz dahin
	goo (AE sl)	sticky liquid	Schmiere, Schleim
	her eyes popped in delight	her eyes opened wide with joy	vor Freude traten ihr fast die Augen über
	to turn red with envy	to blush because sb else gets sth one likes	vor Neid rot werden
	"She walks in beauty ..."	poem by George Gordon Noel Lord Byron, romantic English poet (1788–1824)	
	to cover up	to hide	zudecken
	forgetfulness	inability to remember	Vergesslichkeit
	clime	region	Gegend
	aspect ['--]	appearance	Erscheinung
97	to squeal	to shriek	quietschen
	ashen-faced	very pale	aschfahl
	jealousy ['dʒeləsɪ]	fear to lose a partner to sb else	Eifersucht

	Drifters	50s pop-band	
	intertwined	in close embrace	ineinander verflochten
	to trip	to lose o's balance	stolpern
	tipsy	slightly drunk	beschwipst
	innumerable	uncountable	unzählbar
	to down	to empty a glass fast	runterkippen

CHAPTER 10

98	to clutch	to hold tight	festhalten
	to loosen up ['lu:sn]	to become more relaxed	locker werden, „auftauen"
	booze (infml)	alcohol	Schnaps
	tangled	with arms and legs in a knot	verschlungen
	giant ['dʒaɪənt]	huge	gigantisch
	to pant	to try hard to catch one's breath	keuchen
	shin	front bone of the lower leg	Schienbein
	to pin sb in place	to keep sb firm in place	jdn festnageln
	artificial respiration	treatment for people unable to breathe	künstliche Beatmung
	ward	hospital department	Station
99	to check on	to have a closer look at	sich genauer anschauen
	to throb	to beat	heftig schlagen

	his head was spinning	he was totally confused	ihm drehte sich alles im Kopf
	gorgeous	magnificent	großartig
	outline	profile	Umriss
	nape of one's neck	back of one's neck	Nacken
	contorted	twisted	verzerrt
	agony	extreme suffering	Qual
	temptation	immoral wish	Versuchung
100	to stroke	to rub tenderly	streicheln
	to caress [-'-]	to stroke lovingly	liebkosen
	fabulous	fantastic	fabelhaft
	secretive ['---]	suggesting a secret	geheimnisvoll
101	to flick on	to go on quickly	aufleuchten
	to shield from	to protect against	abschirmen vor
	to smash	to hit hard	schmettern, fest schlagen
	to swing at	to hit hard at	mit Schwingern schlagen nach
	to bang on	to pound on	trommeln auf
	limp	powerless	schlaff
	bruised [bru:zd]	showing the effect of hits	blutunterlaufen
102	to be convened	to be in session	tagen
	adoration	deep love and respect	Anbetung
	to nod	to bow one's head	nicken

	to get lost (sl)	to leave	abhauen
	to catch on (caught, -) (infml)	to understand	kapieren
	to elbow	to hit with the elbow	anstoßen
	to get the hint	to understand	verstehen
	baffled	confused	verwirrt
	dagger	long knife	Dolch
103	to brush	to touch lightly in passing	streifen
	to blink	to shut and open o's eyes quickly	blinzeln
	to be appreciated for [ə'pri:ʃɪeɪtɪd]	to be taken seriously and admired for	geschätzt werden wegen
	"Let me not to the marriage of true minds …"	from "Sonnet CXVI" by William Shakespeare	
	marriage	legal connection between a couple; union	Ehe; Verbindung
	impediment [-'---]	sth that stops you	Hindernis
	to recite a poem	to quote a poem	ein Gedicht rezitieren
104	to alter	to change	sich ändern
	alteration	act of changing	Veränderung
	to bend (bent, -)	here: to turn into a new direction	
	with the remover to remove	i. e. if the beloved person goes away	

satisfaction	emotional well-being	Befriedigung
fixed	set	festgesetzt
tempest	storm	Sturm
bark	type of sailing-ship	Barke
to take the height of a star	to measure the position of a star in the sky	die Höhe eines Sternes messen (zur Positions-bestimmung)
student body	all the students	Studentenschaft
to summon	to call together	zusammenrufen
buzz	sound of many low voices	Summen, Gemurmel
to drone	here: to be audible	ertönen, hörbar sein
swollen	here: distorted from bruises	ge-, verschwollen
drawn with exhaustion [ɪɡ'zɔ:stʃn]	showing extreme tiredness	von Erschöpfung gezeichnet
to stifle a yawn	to suppress a yawn	ein Gähnen unterdrücken
briefcase	small satchel	Kollegmappe
All set!	Everything's ready!	Alles klar!
unauthorized	without official permission	nicht genehmigt
profane	attacking set rules	respektlos
rather than spend …	before I spend …	bevor ich … verbringe

	to ferret out	to try to find	aufspüren
	a guilty party	here: person who has done sth wrong	Schuldige(r)
	to assure sb	to confirm sb	jdm versichern
	expulsion	being forced to leave	Verweisung; Vertreibung
	response	answer	Antwort
	brisk	quick	rasch
	outrageous	causing public anger	empörend, unerhört
	undaunted	fearless	unerschrocken
	to answer the phone	to pick up the phone	den Anruf annehmen
	beet (AE)		rote Bete
	to screech	to yell in an uncontrolled voice	kreischen, schreien
	receiver	part of phone	Hörer
106	blast of laughter	explosion of laughter	Riesengelächter
	stunt	sensational action	Glanznummer; Streich
	smirk	silly smile	Grinsen
	to be involved in sth	to be a part in sth	in etwas verwickelt sein
	to insert	to put in	einfügen
	Assume the position!	Take up the usual position!	Nimm die Stellung ein!
	paddle	wide piece of wood	Paddel

	to drill a hole	to make a hole	ein Loch bohren
	to speed	to make faster	beschleunigen
	progress ['--]	forward movement	Vorwärtsbewegung
	to slam	to hit hard	mit aller Kraft schlagen
	buttocks (pl)	part of the body on which one sits	Gesäß
	to deliver	to send to the right place	austeilen
	lick (AE)	beat	Schlag
	barely (adv)	hardly	kaum
	outer office	secretary's room in front of main office	Vorzimmer
	to proceed	to go on	fortschreiten
	adjacent [ə'dʒeɪsnt]	situated right next	angrenzend
	easel	structure holding a painting	Staffelei
107	moose [mu:s]	American elk	Elch
	awe	combination of fear and respect	Ehrfurcht
	hoarse	rough	heiser
	to make sth up	to invent sth	etwas erfinden
	to expel sb	to drive sb out	jdn verweisen, vertreiben
	to remain enrolled	to remain on the roll of students	eingeschrieben bleiben an der Schule/Universität

	humiliation [hju:ˌmɪlɪˈeɪʃn]	act of taking sb's self-respect	Demütigung
	to forgive (-gave, -given)	to pardon	vergeben
	provided	under the condition	vorausgesetzt
	apology	asking for pardon	Entschuldigung (-srede)
	to mill around	to walk around restlessly	herumlaufen
108	to be kicked out (infml)	to be fired	rausgeschmissen werden
	to turn sb in (infml)	to give away sb's name	jdn verraten
	loaded	meaningful	viel sagend
	to scurry	to walk with short and fast steps	flitzen
109	nostalgic	dreaming of the past	wehmütig
	way before (infml)	here: long before	lang vor
	straight (adv)	directly	direkt
	unorthodox	unusual	ungewöhnlich
	outburst	sudden expression of emotions	Ausbruch
	impressionable	easily impressed	beeindruckbar
	reprimand [ˈreprɪmaːnd]	scolding	Tadel
	evil	here: bad side	Übel
	curriculum [kəˈrɪkjʊləm]	list of things taught	Curriculum, Lehrplan

	to be set	to be fixed	festgesetzt sein
	to prevent sb from doing sth	to keep sb from doing sth	jdn davon abhalten, etwas zu tun
	proven [pru:vn]	tested and found good	bewährt
	patronizing ['pæ-]	acting from a higher position	herablassend
	The rest will take care of itself.	The rest will come automatically.	Der Rest kommt dann schon von allein.
110	hallowed [æ]	sacred	geheiligt
	to raise	to bring up, educate	heranziehen
	confirmed	unmoving	überzeugt, eingefleischt
	rigid	strict	starr
	upbringing	education	Erziehung
	to side with sb	to support sb	auf der Seite von … sein
	in disbelief	unbelievingly	ungläubig
	daring	courageous action	Wagemut
	to be called for	to be necessary at a certain time	angebracht, nötig sein
111	Keep your heads about you!	Don't lose your heads!	Verliert nicht den Kopf!
	to scrawl	to write in a bad hand	kritzeln
	bold	here: thick	hier: fett
	to consider	to look at	betrachten
	indispensable [,--'--]	of the greatest importance	unerlässlich

	dissection	detailed analysis	Detailanalyse
	criticism ['----]	act of criticizing	Kritik
	to expose sb to sth	to show sb sth	jdn einer Sache aussetzen
	transcendent [-'--]	of eternal importance	erhaben, zeitlos
	to devour [aʊ]	to eat in big bites	verschlingen
	utter	total	völlig
	dreck (Yidd sl)	worthless stuff	Schund
	plague [pleɪg]		Pest
112	entitled	bearing the tittle	betitelt
	touching	moving	anrührend
	final paper	end-term test	Abschlussarbeit
	debutante ['debju:ta:nt]	girl being presented to society at a ball	Debütantin
	generously (adv)	in the broadest sense	umfassend
	to volunteer for	to do a task out of o's own free will	sich freiwillig melden für
	combat	battle	Schlacht, Kampf
	sewage ['sju:ɪdʒ]	polluted water of a house or town	Abwasser
	to despair	to become desperate	verzweifeln
	F	lowest grade in school	durchgefallen, „sechs"
	jacket	paper cover of a book	Umschlag
	to sacrifice	to give up	opfern

	to provide sb with sth	to give sb sth	jdm etwas zur Verfügung stellen
	debut [ˈdeɪbuː]	first official presentation	Debüt
	to desire	to wish deeply	sich ersehnen
	to disclaim sth	to deny	abstreiten
	need	necessity	Notwendigkeit
	to restate	to reformulate	nochmals formulieren
	plot	chain of events in a fictional text	Handlungsablauf
	to regurgitate [rɪˈgɜːdʒɪteɪt]	to produce the contents of one's stomach	wieder hochbringen
	to convince sb	to make sb believe	jdn davon überzeugen
	pretentious	claiming importance	hochgestochen
113	dire	horrible	schauderhaft
	Freudian theory	psychological theory of Sigmund Freud (1856–1939)	
	Electra	in Greek mythology woman supposed to have had a love affair with her father	
	Oedipus [ˈiːdɪpəs]	in Greek mythology man who without his knowledge married his mother	
	to skip to	to leave out	auslassen
	obscure n	sth undefinable, secretive	Unergründliches, Dunkles

	to elaborate	to formulate	formulieren, ausführen
	uncanny	mysterious	geheimnisvoll, verblüffend
	to discard	to give up as useless	beiseite schieben
	to behead	to cut off sb's head	enthaupten
	consummate [-'--]	perfect	vollkommen
	to dare do sth	to risk to do sth	wagen, etwas zu tun
	allusion	indirect mentioning	Anspielung
	to be insightful	to show the understanding of sth	erkenntnisreich sein
	A-Plus	(the top mark at school)	15 Punkte/ „Eins plus"
114	dreadful	terrible	schrecklich
	trap	item to catch animals	Falle
	screen	surface used for showing pictures or films	Leinwand; Bildschirm
	slide	transparent picture	Dia
	Sodom and Gomorrah	biblical cities with a reputation of sin	
	delectable	delicious	köstlich
	level	degree	Grad, Niveau
	distraction	lack of concentration	Ablenkung
	to light up (lit, -)	here: to switch on	einschalten
	to focus	to adjust a lens	scharf stellen

	panties (pl)	lower part of women's underwear	Slip
	to do double takes (infml)	to look twice	zweimal hinschauen
	scanty lingerie ['lænʒəri]	almost too small underwear	knappe Dessous
	tight	from a short distance	nah
115	blowup	larger version of a picture	Vergrößerung
	tantalizing ['----]	tormenting	quälend
	to bob up and down	to move quickly up and down	hoch- und runterzucken
	numb [nʌm]	without feeling	stumpf, betäubt, benommen

CHAPTER 11

116	brisk	refreshing	erfrischend
	to engulf	to cover completely	einhüllen
	foliage ['fəʊlɪɪdʒ]	all the leaves of a tree, bush	Blattwerk
	to blanket	to cover like a blanket	bedecken
	brittle	dry	dürr, spröde
	torrent	storm	Sturm
	hooded down jacket	jacket filled with soft goose feathers and with a cover for o's head	Daunenjacke mit Kapuze

	to howl [aʊ]	to make terrible noises, e. g. likes wolves	heulen
	villain ['vɪlən]	wicked person	Schurke
	drawn and ready	with o's sword drawn and ready to fight	zum Kampf bereit
	Where art thou? (obs)	Where are you?	
	plain	flat	eben
	to boom	to speak loudly	donnern, dröhnen
	to bubble	to speak excitedly	sprudeln
117	theatrical flourish ['flʌrɪʃ]	theatrical gesture	theatralische Geste
	performance	presentation of a play etc. to an audience	Aufführung
	chicken (infml)	coward	Feigling
	We'll try no manhood.	We won't test our strength.	Wir werden keine Kraftprobe machen.
	to bow [baʊ]	to bend forward in greeting	sich verbeugen
	to fence	to fight with a sword against	fechten gegen
118	to bark	to speak shortly and angrily	bellen
	to talk back to sb	to contradict sb	jdm widersprechen
	absurd [əb'sɜ:d]		
	to deceive sb	to tell sb a lie	jdn täuschen
	to get away with sth (infml)	to go unpunished	ungestraft davonkommen

	niece	brother's or sister's daughter	Nichte
	You must be mistaken!	This must be an error!	Sie müssen sich irren!
	liar	sb who tells a lie	Lügner
	to quit	to give up immediately	(sofort) aufhören
119	You will not let me down!	You will not disappoint me!	Du wirst mich nicht enttäuschen!
	suspicious	not trusting sb	misstrauisch
	to perpetuate	to keep alive for ever	verewigen
120	That goes for all of you!	That means all of you!	Das gilt für euch alle!
	to switch	to change from one to the other	tauschen
	What good will that do? (infml)	What can that help?	Was bringt das?
	Are you kidding?	Are you joking?	Machst du einen Scherz?
	objection	expression of disagreement	Widerspruch
	quarters (pl)	area where certain people live	Wohnbezirk
121	to plead	to beg urgently	dringend bitten
	to shift on one's feet	to change from one foot to the other	von einem Bein aufs andere treten
	tattered	worn from usage	zerfleddert
	radiant ['reɪdjənt]	brilliant	strahlend

	poor	unsatisfactory	unzureichend
	imagination	power of vision	Phantasie
	dim	weak	schwach
	substitute	(poorer) alternative	Ersatz
122	to creak open	to open noisily	sich quietschend öffnen
	to back away from	to move backwards from	von … zurücktreten
	to worship [ɜ:]	to adore	anbeten
	bureau (AE) ['bjʊərəʊ]	chest of drawers (BE: big desk)	Kommode; Schreibtisch
	to rifle through	to search hastily	durchwühlen
	Drop by any time! (infml)	Come for a short visit whenever you want!	Ihr könnt jederzeit wieder reinschauen!
123	to punch	to knock	boxen
	He couldn't help smiling.	He simply had to smile.	Er konnte sich ein Lächeln nicht verkneifen.
	gosh! (AE sl)	(expression of surprise)	Mensch!
	to smile wryly	to show a twisted smile	schief lächeln
	I can see my father's point.	I understand what my father means.	Ich kann meinen Vater verstehen.
124	to observe	to make a commenting remark	feststellen
	anxious ['æŋkʃəs]	worried	besorgt
	whim	momentary feeling	Laune

	frivolous ['---]	worthless	wertlos, nichtig
	to forget about sth	to stop thinking about sth	sich etwas aus dem Kopf schlagen
	commitment	loving support	Engagement
	to stay true to o. s.	to stick to o's principles	sich selbst treu bleiben
	to scatter	to spread all over	sich verstreuen
	to call a meeting to order	to open a meeting officially	eine Sitzung offiziell eröffnen
125	curfew ['kɜ:fju:]	time when one has to be back	Ausgangssperre, Zapfenstreich
	if we don't beat it (AE sl)	if we don't leave fast	wenn wir uns nicht gleich auf die Socken machen
126	to plot a scheme [ski:m]	to make a plan	einen Plan aushecken
	plowed (AE; BE: ploughed) [plaʊd]	here: freed from snow	hier: (vom Schnee) geräumt
	to speed away (sped, -)	to drive/ride away fast	davonbrausen, -flitzen
	frantically (adv)	desperately	wie rasend
	to bustle about [bʌsl]	to move about fast in a chaos	herumwimmeln
	he double-timed it	he ran like a flash	er sprintete
127	bouquet [bʊ'keɪ]	bunch of flowers	Blumenstrauß
	wilted	slightly dried	verwelkt

	frostbitten	damaged by frost	erfroren
	to deserve better	to be worthy of sth better	etwas Besseres verdienen
	to bug sb (AE infml)	to get on sb's nerves	jdn nerven
	drooping	hanging downwards	herabhängend
128	to restrain	to suppress	unterdrücken
	contentment	satisfaction, happiness	Zufriedenheit

Chapter 12

131	to ditch (sl)	to get rid of	loswerden
	triumphant [traɪ'ʌmfənt]	happy as after a victory	triumphierend
	to help o. s. to	to take (food etc.)	sich bedienen
	sweet roll		Brötchen
	oven ['ʌvn]	part of stove used for baking	Backofen
132	to usher sb into a room	to lead sb into a room	jdn in einen Raum geleiten
	encounter	meeting	Begegnung
	exhilarated [ɪg'zɪləreɪtɪd]	in seventh heaven	überglücklich
	to scamper	to walk fast	hasten
	virility	manlihood	Männlichkeit
133	to faint	to lose o's consciousness	in Ohnmacht fallen
	We'll be in big trouble. (sl)	We'll have big problems.	Wir werden in der Tinte sitzen.

	to barge into (infml)	to come running into	reinplatzen
	to make a fool of sb	to make sb look ridiculous	jdn als Narren dastehen lassen
	over and over (infml)	again and again	immer wieder
	to honk for sb	to blow the horn for sb	wegen jdm hupen
134	just like that (infml)	without thinking	einfach so
	if it so happens that … (infml)	if it were true that …	wenn es aber nun mal so wäre, dass …
	to be infuriating [-’----]	to make sb very angry	jdn rasend machen
	to bow out [baʊ]	to leave for good	sich auf immer verabschieden
	to sneak away	to leave unnoticed	sich hinausschleichen
135	sincere	honest	aufrichtig
	reluctant	against sb’s will	widerstrebend
	he made his grand entrance	he appeared for his big scene	er hatte seinen großen Auftritt
	Whither wander you? (obs)	Where do you go?	
	dale	valley	Tal
	thorough (obs) [’θʌrə]	through	
	fairy	female spirit	Elfe, Fee
	Oberon [’əʊbərən]	king of the fairies in *A Midsummer Night’s Dream*	

	to beguile [bɪ'gaɪl]	to deceive	täuschen
	to neigh [neɪ]	to cry like a horse	wiehern
	filly foal	young female horse	Stutfohlen
	ease	lack of difficulty	Leichtigkeit
	to mouth a line	to speak voicelessly	stumm mitsprechen
136	Lysander, Hermia [laɪ'sændə]	loving couple in *A Midsummer Night's Dream*	
	turf	grassy patch	Rasensode
	bosom ['bʊzəm]	seat of emotions	Busen, „Herz"
	troth (obs) [trəʊθ]	faithfulness	Treue
	nay (obs)	no	
	for my sake	because of me	um meinetwillen
	courtesy ['kɜ:tɪsɪ]	politeness	Höflichkeit
	modesty	being satisfied with what one is/has	Bescheidenheit
	separation	not being together	Trennung
	sth becomes sb	sth suits sb	etwas steht jdm gut
	virtuous	morally good	tugendhaft
	bachelor ['bætʃələ]	unmarried man	Junggeselle
	enraptured	fascinated	hingerissen
	wings (pl)	side decorations of a stage	Seitenkulissen

137	character	person in a drama	Gestalt
	musical interlude	music played between acts	musikalisches Zwischenspiel
	revelry	feasting, merrymaking	Fest, Lustbarkeit
	uninhibited	free and spontaneous	unbefangen
	slow motion	slowed-down action	Zeitlupe
	spellbound	tied down by a magic spell	gebannt, verzaubert
	awed by [ɔ:d]	filled with respect and wonder	ergriffen von
	rapture	total fascination	Verzückung
	to become infatuated with sb [-'----]	to fall deeply in love with sb	sich in jdn vernarren
	to address [-'-]	to speak to	sprechen zu
	to offend	to hurt sb's feelings	beleidigen
	to mend	here: to set right	regeln
	but (adv)	here: only	
	to slumber	to sleep lightly	schlummern
	idle	meaningless	bedeutungslos
	to reprehend [,--'-]	to blame	tadeln
138	to scape (obs)	to escape	
	serpent	snake	Schlange
	to make amends	to pay for harm or damage done	Schadenersatz leisten

	ere long (obs)	before long	
	Robin (Goodfellow)	other name for Puck	
	to restore amends	to compensate for a damage	den Schaden wieder gutmachen
	to dispel doubt	to rid of uncertainties	Zweifel zerstreuen
	actor	man acting in a play	Schauspieler
	to rise to a standing ovation (rose, risen)	to rise to applaud	sich zu stehendem Beifall erheben
	to follow suit	to do the same as sb else	es gleichtun
	curtain call	extra applause for a certain actor/actress	„Vorhang“
	to take o's bows	to bow to the audience	sich verbeugen (als Schauspieler o. ä.)
	cast	all the actors	Besetzung, Mitwirkende
	to mingle with	to mix with	sich unter … mischen
	to be mobbed	to be densely surrounded	umringt, belagert sein
	well-wisher	person congratulating	Gratulant, Anhänger
139	backstage	behind the stage	hinter der Bühne
	dressing room	room where actors change clothes	Garderobe
	jubilant	overjoyed	jubelnd
	celebration	festivities	Feiern

	headpiece	head-decoration	Kopfschmuck
	to sense	to feel	spüren
140	to burst open (-, -)	to open quickly	aufspringen
	throng	crowd	Menschenmenge
	It's no use!	It won't help!	Es hat keinen Sinn!
	stunned	paralysed	gelähmt
141	chilled with sympathy	with a shiver of sympathy	vor Mitgefühl erschauernd

CHAPTER 13

142	stuffy	full of things	voll gestopft
	study	room for paperwork	Arbeitszimmer
	to defy sb	to resist sb	jdm trotzen
	to withdraw sb	to take sb away	hier: jdn abmelden
	to enrol sb	to send sb to a school	jdn anmelden
	bloodshot eyes	eyes with the blood vessels visible	blutunterlaufene Augen
143	to squander [ɒ]	to waste	vergeuden
	drained of emotion	unable to feel anything	aller Gefühle entleert
	to lay out	to plan	planen
144	he poked his head in	he looked in	er streckte seinen Kopf herein
	to second a motion	to support an idea put to a meeting	einen Antrag unterstützen

	to relent	to give in	einlenken
	e. e. cummings	(= Edward Eslin) Cummings, American poet (1894–1962)	
	to dive for	to swim under water for	tauchen nach
	to topple	to turn over	umwerfen
146	to heed	to pay attention	Acht geben
	to dodge	to get around, evade	ausweichen, umgehen
	savio(u)r	person who saves sb	Retter, Erlöser
	salvation	rescue from sin or danger	Rettung, Heil
	modest	without much ado	bescheiden
	to pluck	to pull and break	pflücken
	spherical ['sferɪkl]	ball-shaped	rund
	icicle ['aɪsɪkl]	pointed piece of ice	Eiszapfen
147	to intone	to speak solemnly	feierlich sprechen
	to draw apart (drew, drawn)	to split up	sich trennen
	"General William Booth Enters into Heaven"	poem by Vachel Lindsay, American poet and graphic designer (1879–1931)	
	bass drum [beɪs]	large drum with a deep sound	Basstrommel
	to pay sb homage ['hɒmidʒ]	to do sth in sb's honour	jdm huldigen

	limbs (pl) [lɪmz]	legs and arms	Glieder
	shell	hard outer part e. g. of a nut, egg or sea animal	Schale, Muschel
	to be crushed by sth	to be destroyed by sth	zerquetscht werden von etwas

Chapter 14

148	in abundance	in great numbers	im Überfluss
	freeze	frost	Frost
	sparkling	shining with many small lights	funkelnd
	grave	serious	gewichtig
	leper [ˈlepə]		Leprakranker
	bravo [ˈbra:vəʊ]	murderer	(Meuchel-)Mörder
	ditch	long hole in the ground	Graben
	dank	wet and cold	feuchtkalt
	drab	prostitute	Hure
	alleyway [ˈ---]	narrrow passage between houses	Häuserdurchgang
	drug fiend [fi:nd]	drug addict	Drogensüchtiger
	passion ridden	full of passion	von Leidenschaft besessen
	frail	weakened	geschwächt
	ominous [ˈ---]	mysterious	geheimnisvoll

	to settle over	to cover	sich legen über
149	law of gravity	one of Isaac Newton's theories	Schwerkraftgesetz
	to bounce off sth	to be reflected by	zurückgeworfen werden
	to cast (-, -)	to throw	werfen
	mystical	full of spiritual importance	mystisch, geheimnisvoll
150	frantic	wild	ungestüm
	to drift away	to move slowly away	wegtreiben, weggleiten
	robe (AE)	garment worn over pyjamas	Morgenrock
	to flail	to move o's arms intensively	herumfuchteln
	glistening ['glɪsnɪŋ]	shining	glänzend
	to gasp	to breathe with difficulty	nach Luft schnappen
	anguished ['æŋgwɪʃt]	tormented	gequält
151	to be wiped (AE sl)	to be totally worn out	völlig kaputt sein
	to squint	to look with halfclosed eyes	mit zusammengekniffenen Augen schauen
	to vomit	to throw up food	sich übergeben
	guts (pl)	contents of the belly	Eingeweide

	stall	small room	Kabine
152	to pull the trigger	to shoot	den Abzug betätigen
	sob	weeping sound	Schluchzer
	to leave sb alone	not to bother sb	jdn in Ruhe lassen
	grief	great sorrow	Kummer
	somber (AE; BE: sombre)	dark	düster
	bleak	cold and cheerless	trostlos
	to whip	to blow sharply	peitschen
	lament [-ˈ -]	wailing	Klagen
	veiled [veɪld]	wearing a transparent cloth in front of o's face	verschleiert
153	chaplain [ˈtʃæplɪn]	priest	Kaplan, Geistlicher
	grant us the grace	fulfil our deep wish	gewähre uns die Gunst
	to entrust to	to give into the care of	anvertrauen
	never-failing	never-ending	nie versagend
	countenance [ˈ---]	face	Antlitz
	gracious	forgiving	gnädig
	forevermore	forever	für immer, immerdar
	concerned	worried	betroffen, beunruhigt

	at the request of	because ... has asked	auf Bitten von ...
	to conduct an inquiry into sth	to investigate	eine Untersuchung durchführen über
	to reassemble [,ri:ə'sembl]	to meet again	sich wieder versammeln
	trunk room	room for suitcases	Gepäckraum
	basement	AE: ground floor	Keller
154	We're fried! (AE sl)	They are catching us!	Wir sind geliefert!
	fink (AE sl)	sb who informs the authorities	„Singvögelchen", Verräter
	to fink (AE sl)	to inform the authorities	verpfeifen
	scapegoat	person taking the blame	Sündenbock
155	dumbo (AE sl)	stupid guy	Blödmann
	in case	if	für den Fall, dass ...
	hono(u)r code	set of moral rules	Ehrenkodex
	rat (infml)	sb working with the enemy	elender Verräter
156	to put sb up to sth	to encourage sb to do sth bad or criminal	jdn zu etwas anstiften
	if it wasn't for him	had he not been	wenn er nicht gewesen wäre
	cozied up (infml)	comfortable	gemütlich
	Let K. fry! (AE sl)	Let K. be punished!	Laß K. dran glauben!

	to strike sb in the jaw (struck, -)	to hit sb at the chin	jdm einen Kinnhaken geben
	to straddle sb	to sit on sb with a leg on either side	rittlings auf jdm sitzen

Chapter 15

157	stripped	without its covering	abgezogen
	to be escorted	to be officially accompanied	eskortiert werden
158	on the verge of [vɜːdʒ]	very close to	am Rande von, nah
	shaken	confused and sad	erschüttert
	to huff and puff (infml)	to breath hard with exhaustion	schnaufen und keuchen
	strain	effort	Anstrengung
159	gallows (pl)	construction for hanging people	Galgen
	grim	bitter	grimmig
	perspiration	sweat	Schweiß
	brow [braʊ]	side of one's head	Schläfe
	to stain	to leave a spot	beflecken
	reckless	without caring about others	rücksichtslos
	self-indulgent	without limitations	zügellos
160	obsession	fixed idea taking up all o's attention	fixe Idee, Manie

	explicit [-'--]	clear	klar, deutlich
	blatant [eɪ]	unashamed	schamlos, dreist
	abuse [ə'bju:s]	unjustified use	Missbrauch
	to amend [-'-]	to correct	berichtigen, ergänzen
	to prosecute sb ['---]	to start legal action against sb	jdn strafrechtlich verfolgen
	to guarantee sth [--'-]	to promise sth officially	garantieren
	to see to it that	to make sure that	dafür sorgen, dass
	for our sakes	for us	um unseretwillen
161	What do you care?	Why does it bother you?	Was kümmerst du dich darum?
	to suffer the consequences	to feel the results	die Folgen tragen
	disciplinary probation	test period for sb's proper behaviour	Bewährung aus Disziplingründen
	to do work duty	to do extra work as a punishment	Strafarbeiten verrichten
162	We'll bring him around.	We'll get him on the right path again.	Wir bringen ihn wieder auf den rechten Weg.
	teachers' residence floor	floor in a dorm where teachers live	Lehrerflur
	to resume doing sth	to take up doing sth	wieder anfangen mit
	conspicuously (adv)	catching o's eye	auffällig

163	to take over sth	to assume the responsibility for sth from sb	übernehmen
	to fumble	to play with one's hands	herumfummeln
	exasperated [-'----]	annoyed	gereizt
	to cover	to talk about	durchnehmen
	post-Civil War	after 1865	
	to skip	to leave out	überspringen
	We'll start over. (AE)	We'll begin once more.	Wir fangen noch mal von vorn an.
	personals (AE pl)	personal belongings	Privatsachen
	testy	irritated	gereizt
164	closet (AE) ['--]	built-in wardrobe	Wandschrank
165	enraged	furious	wütend, außer sich
	to shriek	to scream in a shrill voice	schreien, kreischen
	to take sb in	to look at sb from head to toe	jdn von oben bis unten mustern
	to prop up a foot	to put a foot on sth as a support	einen Fuß stützen
	to hoist o. s. up	to pull o. s. up	sich hinaufziehen
166	to muster up one's courage	to take all one's courage	seinen ganzen Mut aufbieten
	tribute ['--]	expression of deep respect	Huldigung

Topics and Tasks for Analysis

Chapter 1 (1–8)

- You have participated in the welcoming ceremony of Welton Academy now. What are your first impressions of that school and its teachers?
- Describe and discuss the "four pillars" of Welton Academy. Could you think of alternative principles/values?
- Describe your first impressions of Todd, Knox, Charlie, Neil, and Cameron.
- What does the reaction of the parents reveal about the relationships with their sons?
- After reading the first chapter, speculate about possible themes and conflicts in the novel.
- Check history books and encyclopaedias and try to get information about the USA in 1959 and the years around.

Chapter 2 (9–14)

- Which additional information do you get about the boys?
- How do you see the relationship within their group?
- What impression of the atmosphere at Welton Academy have you got so far?

Chapter 3 (15–19)

- How does Mr. Perry treat his son? What do you think about his methods?
- How do the other boys react to the confrontation?
- Compare Todd's and Neil's situation.
- Try to explain why Neil jabs his thumb with a pin.

Chapter 4 (20–27)

- Describe the students' first lessons in chemistry, Latin and maths. What is your opinion about the methods used by their teachers?
- How does Mr. Keating's teaching style differ from that of his colleagues?
- Which means does he use to motivate the students?
- Describe their reaction.
- Keating invites the boys to call him "O Captain! My Captain!". Could you imagine why? Support your view by looking up Whitman's poem.
- What does Keating mean by "Carpe Diem"? Explain.
- Imagine one of your teachers behaved like John Keating. How would you react?

Chapter 5 (28–42)

- How does Todd feel about the new school?
- Describe Knox's visit at the Danburrys'. How does he react when he sees Chris?
- How does J. Evan Pritchard rate poetry? Do you think his method is useful?
- According to Keating, what is the importance of poetry? Do you share his view? What does poetry/literature mean to you?
- Look up in an encyclopaedia what you can find about William Wordsworth's notion of romanticism and try to collect information about Walt Whitman and his poem *Leaves of Grass*.

Chapter 6 (43–50)

- How do Keating's colleagues react to his unconventional methods?

- What does Keating tell the boys about the "Dead Poets Society"?
- Why do they want to recreate that secret group?
- Taking Chapter 1 to 6 into account, try to characterize Keating. Do his aims and methods appeal to you? Does he qualify as a 'good' teacher? Discuss.
- In preparation for the next chapter, try to get information about Henry David Thoreau and *Walden*.

CHAPTER 7 (51–66)

- Describe the refoundation of the Dead Poets Society.
- Explain the "opening message" from Thoreau's *Walden* (p. 53). What does it suggest? Why does ist, like the other literary quotations, appeal to the boys?
- Keating says that language was invented "to woo women". Discuss his thesis in class.
- Keating tries to teach the boys to find their "own voice" (p. 61). Do you consider this as a main educational aim? Could you think of other objectives that are just as important for one's personal development?
- Explain Neil's decision to act in a play. Speculate about possible consequences.
- How does Neil manage to get Todd into the Dead Poets Society?

CHAPTER 8 (67–80)

- Explain why Keating combines his soccer instruction with poetry and the rhythm of classical music.
- Is there a common idea in the quotations Keating has chosen? Discuss.
- Comment on his thesis that "the most important thing in all sport is the way other human beings push us to excel" (p. 70).

- According to Keating, poetry ist not restricted to the word but inherent in many aspects of life. Do you agree with this view or do you think it is too idealistic? Discuss in class.
- Describe how Keating teaches Todd to overcome his self-consciousness and to find his own poetic voice. Could you think of alternative ways of giving him confidence?
- How is the act of creating poetry presented in this scene?
- Keating's ideas have also affected Charlie. Describe how he has changed.
- In preparation for the following chapter, try to get information about William Shakespeare and his play *A Midsummer Night's Dream.*

Chapter 9 (81–97)

- What does Todd's unwanted birthday present reveal about the relationship between him and his parents? What futher information do we get about the position he has in his family?
- Keating quotes a few lines from Robert Frost's poem "The Road Not Taken". What is the purpose of this experiment? What is your your opinion about it?
- Read the poem and show how it is linked with Keating's philosophy.
- Explain the significance of Charlie's changing his name to 'Nuwanda'.
- Keating tells the boys that language was invented "to woo women". How does Charlie put this idea into practice? What do you think of the way he treats the two girls?
- What happens to Knox during the party at the Danburys'?
- What is the function and effect of alternating between two different scenes in the second part of this chapter?

Chapter 10 (98–115)

- Describe the circumstances and consequences of Knox's amorous advances to Chris.
- What practical joke does Charlie play during the assembly?
- How is he punished by Nolan?
- How does Charlie react to Nolan's request that he should apologize and inform on the Dead Poets Society?
- Compare Nolan's and Keating's teaching aims as shown in their conversation. Do you share Nolan's view that the boys are too young to think for themselves?
- In this chapter, Mr. McAllister comments on Keating's educational methods again. What part does he play in the novel?
- How does Keating introduce his students to college? Do you think they will profit from this introduction? Discuss in class.
- What is your impression of Keating in this chapter? Is his behaviour convincing? Discuss.

Chapter 11 (116–129)

- How does Neil feel during his rehearsal for *A Midsummer Night's Dream*?
- Describe his father's reaction. What do you think of the arguments he puts forward?
- What do the boys find out about Keating's private life when they are in his room? How does he react to their visit?
- Do you think Keating's advice to Neil will help the boy to solve his problems? Explain your view.
- How does Knox try to win Chris's love? What do you think about his tactics and the poem itself?

Chapter 12 (130–141)

- For what reasons may Neil not have told Keating the truth?
- How does the relationship between Chris and Knox develop?
- What reactions does the performance of *A Midsummer Night's Dream* produce in the audience?
- Analyse Neil's closing monologue and show how it is thematically linked with reality.
- Describe the general atmosphere at the end of this chapter. What means does the author use to heighten the dramatic effect?
- Read/act out Neil's departure from the group, trying to express how the different characters may have felt in this scene.

Chapter 13 (142–147)

- How does Mr Perry react to Neil's disobedience?
- Describe the mood of the boys before Keating arrives.
- Do you think the poem by e. e. cummings is well-chosen in this situation? Explain your view.

Chapter 14 (148–156)

- At the beginning of Chapter 14 you find a sequence of alternating scenes set in the Perrys' house and in the wood. What is the dramatic effect achieved by this technique?
- Neil's suicide is being parallelled by the "revelry" of the boys in the wood. Can you find any thematic links and symbolic elements in this sequence?
- How do Keating and the boys react to Neil's death?

- Describe and discuss the behaviour of the boys during the investigation. Does Cameron's betrayal come as a surprise to you?

CHAPTER 15 (157–166)

- How do Meeks and Knox behave during Nolan's interrogation?
- Read the passage about Todd's interrogation aloud and explain his response to Nolan's demand to sign the incrimatory paper.
- Comment on the picture Nolan draws of Keating in this paper.
- Discuss the significance of Nolan's choosing the "excellent" Pritchard essay when taking Keating's English lesson.
- Before Keating leaves, the boys stand up on their desks "in silent salute" to their teacher. Explain the deeper significance of this scene.
- Imagine Keating keeps a diary. Write a short entry about the final scene from Keating's point of view. Do not forget to describe the thoughts and feelings that may have come into his mind.

NOW THAT YOU HAVE FINISHED READING THE BOOK

- Imagine it is Neil's funeral. One of Neil's friends speaks on behalf of the Dead Poets Society commemorating their dead friend. Write a speech for him.
- The year is 1960. The students are preparing a new yearbook and Mr. Nolan wants to put in an obituary for Neil. What could he write?
- Imagine a trial about the death of Neil. Who is to blame for it? What can you say for or against Neil's parents, Dean Nolan, and Mr. Keating?

- Which of the boys do you find most interesting? Explain your view.
- Describe the development you see in the characters of Neil, Todd, and Charlie.
- Which part do girls/women play in the book?
- Mr. Keating: an ideal teacher, a demagogue, a dreamer, a ... ? What is your view of him?
- Would you recommend this book to other pupils? Give a speech in which you either recommend or advise against reading it.

If you have seen the film

- Where are the main differences between the book and the film? Check especially the opening scene, Chapter 8 (Todd's "barbaric YAWP"), the description of Neil's suicide, the investigation in Nolan's office, and the final scene.
  What may be reasons for these differences?
- Did the actors conform to the image you had of the main characters when reading the book? Are they the right types and age? Do you think they ought to look different? Explain your view.
- Which means does the director use to create a certain mood/atmosphere in the film?
- Is the atmosphere created in the film the same as the one in the book? Discuss.
- What did you enjoy more, the book or the film? Why?

Additional Texts

POETS, DEAD AND YET ALIVE …

One of the aims of Mr. Keating's teaching and the Dead Poets Society is to revive classical poetry. He wants to show that these poets are not really dead but have only been quiet for a while and are now coming back to life in the people who read them.

We hope that you will agree after you have read the poems we have chosen.

A poem in memory of President Lincoln

Abraham Lincoln (1809–1865) was the president during whose term of office the only civil war in the history of the USA was fought (1861–65). The eleven Confederate States of the South had declared their independence from the Union because they wanted to keep slavery for their plantations and feared the superiority of the Northern industries.

Lincoln managed to force the Southern States back into the Union. On September 22, 1862 he declared all slaves in the Confederate States to be free. The war ended on May 26, 1865 after 600 000 people had been killed and more than one million wounded.

Abraham Lincoln did not see the end of the war any more. On April 14, 1865 he was shot in the head and killed by a fanatic.

O Captain! My Captain! by Walt Whitman

O Captain! my Captain! our fearful trip is done,
The ship has weather'd every rack, the prize we sought is won,

The port is near, the bells I hear, the people all exulting,
While follow eyes the steady keel, the vessel grim and daring;
But O heart! heart! heart!
O the bleeding drops of red,
Where on the deck my Captain lies,
Fallen cold and dead.

O Captain! my Captain! rise up and hear the bells;
Rise up – for you the flag is flung – for you the bugle trills,
For you bouquets and ribbon'd wreaths – for you the shores a-crowding,
For you they call, the swaying mass, their eager faces turning;
Here Captain! dear father!
This arm beneath your head!
It is some dream that on the deck,
You've fallen cold and dead.

My Captain does not answer, his lips are pale and still,
My father does not feel my arm, he has no pulse nor will,
The ship is anchor'd safe and sound, its voyage closed and done,
From fearful trip the victor ship comes in with object won;
Exult O shores, and ring O bells!
But I with mournful tread,
Walk the deck my Captain lies,
Fallen cold and dead.

(originally 1865–6, revised 1871)

From: Sculley Bradley, Harold W. Blodgett (ed.)
Walt Whitman, *Leaves of Grass*, New York: Norton, 1973, 337f.

2 ***to weather a rack*** to survive a storm; *3* ***to exult*** to sing with joy; *4* ***steady keel*** (steter Kurs) • ***vessel*** ship; *10* ***bugle*** ['bju:gl] signal trumpet • ***to trill*** to sound; *11* ***ribboned wreaths*** (bandverzierte Kränze); *12* ***to sway*** to move from one side to the other; *19 **to win an object*** to reach an aim; *22 **tread*** step

POINTS FOR ANALYSIS AND DISCUSSION

- What picture of Abraham Lincoln does Walt Whitman convey to the reader?
- Analyse the arrangement of images and ideas in this poem. What do you notice about the repetitions of words and sentence patterns, the length and order of lines? What is the effect of these formal elements?
- How does the rhythmical pattern of the poem underline what Whitman wants to say?
- What do we learn about Mr. Keating when he wants to be called "O Captain! my Captain!"?

A book in praise of the autonomous individual

Walt Whitman's long poem *Leaves of Grass* was published for the first time in 1855 and then permanently revised and added to until Whitman's death in 1892. In free rhythm and by creating a profusion of associations Whitman praises American idealism and describes the growth of a new nation independent of its European ancestors.

Poets to Come

Poets to come! orators, singers, musicians to come!
Not to-day is to justify me and answer what I am for,
But you, a new brood, native, athletic, continental, greater
    than before known,
Arouse! for you must justify me.

I myself but write one or two indicative words for the
    future,

Walt Whitman

I but advance a moment only to wheel and hurry back in the darkness.

I am a man who, sauntering along without fully stopping, turns a casual look upon you and then averts his face,
Leaving it to you to prove and define it,
Expecting the main things from you.

(orginally 1860, revised 1867)

From: Bradley/Blodgett, 14

1 orator speaker; *4 to arouse* to wake up; 5 ***indicative*** [-'---] showing the way; 7 ***to saunter*** to walk casually • ***to avert*** [ə'vɜ:t] to turn away

✳

From: **Starting from Paumanok**

5
Dead poets, philosophs, priests,
Martyrs, artists, inventors, governments long since,
Language shapers on other shores,
Nations once powerful, now reduced, withdrawn, or desolate,
I dare not proceed till I respectfully credit what you have left wafted hither,
I have perused it, own it is admirable, (moving awhile among it,)
Think nothing can ever be greater, nothing can ever deserve more than it deserves,
Regarding it all intently a long while, then dismissing it,
I stand in my place with my own day here.

(...)

From: Bradley/Blodgett 15–28, 17f.

Paumanok Long Island; 4 ***desolate*** deserted and miserable; 5 ***to proceed*** to move on • ***to credit*** to add to o's account;

• *wafted* carried by the wind • ***hither*** here; *6* ***to peruse*** to read through • ***to own*** here: to admit; *8* ***to dismiss*** to put aside

*

From: **Song of Myself**

1

I celebrate myself, and sing myself,
And what I assume you shall assume,
For every atom belonging to me as good belongs to you.

I loafe and invite my soul,
I lean and loafe at my ease observing a spear of summer grass.

(...)

52

The spotted hawk swoops by and accuses me, he complains of my gab and my loitering.
I too am not a bit tamed, I too am untranslatable,
I sound my barbaric yawp over the roofs of the world.

(...)

I bequeath myself to the dirt to grow from the grass I love,
If you want me again look for me under your boot-soles.

You will hardly know who I am or what I mean,
But I shall be good health to you nevertheless,
And filter and fibre your blood.

Failing to fetch me at first keep encouraged,
Missing me one place search another,
I stop somewhere waiting for you.

(originally 1855, in 1856 titled "Poem of Walt Whitman, an American")

From: Bradley/Blodgett, 28–89, 28, 89

4 ***to loaf(e)*** to be inactive; *1331* ***to swoop*** to shoot down from the sky • ***gab*** useless chattering • ***to loiter*** to stand around doing nothing; *1339* ***to bequeath*** to pass sth on after o's death

Points for analysis and discussion

- How does Whitman see his place in the chain of poets of the past and the future?
- How does he see the role of the individual in the world?
- What is the relationship between the individual and the future generations?
- Walt Whitman calls his "Song of Myself" a "poem". What ist 'poetic' in "Song of Myself" and the other excerpts from *Leaves of Grass?*
- What makes the passages from Whitman's work so fascinating for Mr. Keating and the boys, and perhaps for you?

A poem in praise of youth

The following poem by Robert Herrick (1591–1674) stands in a long literary tradition. It goes back to the famous poem "De Rosis Nascentibus" ("On Budding Roses") by the Roman poet Decimus Magnus Ausonius (died A. D. 393).

To the Virgins, to Make Much of Time

Gather ye Rose-buds while ye may,
Old Time is still a flying,
And this same flower that smiles to day
To morrow will be dying.

The glorious Lamp of Heaven, the Sun,
The higher he's a getting;

The sooner will his race be run,
And neerer he's to Setting.

That Age is best, which is the first,
When Youth and Blood are warmer;
But being spent, the worse, and worst
Times will succeed the former.

Then be not coy, but use your time;
And while ye may, goe marry:
For having lost but once your prime,
You may for ever tarry.

(1648)

From: John Hayward (ed.), *The Penguin Book of English Verse*, Harmondsworth, 1973, 158f.

virgin woman untouched by a man; *1* ***ye*** (obs) you/your • ***rosebud*** unopened rose blossom; *2* ***still*** here: always; *13* ***coy*** shy *14* ***goe marry*** be merry; *15* ***prime*** time of greatest energy, beauty etc.; *16* ***to tarry*** to wait, hesitate

Points for analysis and discussion

- Which advice does Robert Herrick give the reader?
- Which images does Herrick use for the idea of fleeting time? What do they suggest?
- When reading this poem aloud, you will notice that the rhythmical pattern of the lines sometimes changes. What effect does this have?

A poem in praise of love

William Shakespeare is not only famous as the author of a large number or dramas which are still popular on the stages of the world. He has also written 154 sonnets.

Sonnets are poems which follow strict structural rules. Perhaps you can find them.

Sonnet CXVI

Let me not to the marriage of true minds
Admit impediments. Love is not love
Which alters when it alteration finds,
Or bends with the remover to remove:
O, no! it is an ever-fixéd mark,
That looks on tempests and is never shaken;
It is the star to every wandering bark,
Whose worth's unknown, although his height be taken.
Love's not Time's fool, though rosy lips and cheeks
Within his bending sickle's compass come;
Love alters not with his brief hour and weeks,
But bears it out even to the edge of doom.
  If this be error, and upon me prov'd,
  I never writ, nor no man ever lov'd.

From: W. J. Craig, M. A., *Shakespeare: Complete Works*, London: OUP, 1966, 1122.

1 ***marriage*** legal connection between couple, union; *2* ***impediment*** (Hindernis); *3* ***to alter*** to change • ***alteration*** act of changing; **4 to bend (bent, –)** to turn into a new direction • ***with the remover to remove*** if the beloved person goes away; *5* ***fixed*** set; *6* ***tempest*** storm; *7* ***bark*** sailing ship; *8* ***to take the height of a star*** to navigate by measuring the positions of stars; *10* ***sickle*** (Sichel) • ***compass*** here: circle

Points for analysis and discussion

- Throughout the ages, extravagant claims have been made by lovers and poets for the lasting powers of love. What is your opinion of such claims?

- What arguments are used in the various parts of poem?
- Analyse the structure of the poem. What is the form and function of the last two lines?
- What sections of life are the images taken from? How does their use enhance the force of the speaker's arguments?
- If you had been in Gloria's place, how would you have reacted to the poem?

A poem on steadfastness

The following poem by William Ernest Henley (1849–1903) is perhaps his most famous one. It seems to reflect the poet's attitude after a time of grave personal problems.

Invictus

Out of the night that covers me,
  Black as the Pit from pole to pole,
I thank whatever gods may be
  For my unconquerable soul.

In the fell clutch of circumstance
  I have not winced nor cried aloud.
Under the bludgeonings of chance
  My head is bloody, but unbowed.

Beyond this place of wrath and tears
  Looms but the Horror of the shade,
And yet the menace of the years
  Finds, and shall find, me unafraid.

It matters not how strait the gate,
  How charged with punishments the scroll,
I am the master of my fate:
  I am the captain of my soul.

From: William Butler Yeats (ed.), *Oxford Book of Modern Verse*, Oxford: Clarendon, 1970, p. 25

invictus (Lat) undefeated or undefeatable; *2 pit* access to a mine; *4 unconquerable* undefeatable; *5 fell* cruel • *clutch* tight grip; *7 bludgeoning* [ˈblʌdʒənɪŋ] heavy blow; *10 to loom* to wait threateningly; *11 menace* threat; *13 strait* narrow; *14 charged with* full of • *scroll* (Schriftrolle)

Points for analysis and discussion

- Describe the situation the speaker is in.
- What attitude to his fate does he show?
- Which images are used to emphasize the speaker's attitude to his life and fate?
- Compare the ideas of this poem with those expressed in the excerpts from Whitman's *Leaves of Grass.*

A poem on intellectual independence

Robert Frost (1874–1963) is considered the most-highly praised poet of the United States in the first half of this century. He seems to form a bridge between the New England writers like Thoreau and modern times.

The Road Not Taken

Two roads diverged in a yellow wood,
And sorry I could not travel both
And be one traveler, long I stood
And looked down one as far as I could
To where it bent in the undergrowth;

Then took the other, as just as fair,
And having perhaps the better claim,
Because it was grassy and wanted wear;
Though as for that the passing there

Had worn them really about the same,

And both that morning equally lay
In leaves no step had trodden black.
Oh, I kept the first for another day!
Yet knowing how way leads on to way,
I doubted if I should ever come back.

I shall be telling this with a sigh
Somewhere ages and ages hence:
Two roads diverged in a wood, and I –
I took the one less traveled by,
And that has made all the difference.

(1916)

From: Gerald Dewitt Sanders et al. (ed.), *Chief Modern Poets of England and America,* New York: Macmillan, 1963, II–84

1 ***to diverge*** to fork; *17* ***hence*** from now; *20* ***that makes all the difference*** that is the most important point

Points for analysis and discussion

- What situation does the speaker find himself in?
- What reasons does he give for his choice?
- What are the speaker's feelings about the decision he made?
- Which steps of the speaker's process of decision do the different stanzas show?
- Why could taking the road 'less travelled by' make 'all the difference'?
- If you have an important decision to make, what will you base it on?
- Can you understand the speaker's motivation and reasons for his choice?

SCHOOLS IN THE U.S.A

In the 1980s and 90s there has been a widespread discussion about schools and their quality and aims in the U.S.A.. In 1983 a study was published by the National Commission on Excellence in Education. It had the alarming title *A Nation at Risk: The Imperative for Educational Reform* and demanded immediate action, but the problems don't seem to be solved yet.

In the following chapter you will get information about schools in the U.S.A.. You will find general descriptions, but you will also find articles which deal with problems of the school system and characterize the type of schools like Welton Academy – the prep school.

After this we will concentrate on a certain school – St. Andrew's School in Middletown, Delaware. It is a prep school with a very good standing and – it is the school where the movie *Dead Poets Society* was shot. So we will get insight into a real prep school, from its own materials and forty years after the Dead Poets.

The American School System: Organization and Structure

Education in the United States comprises three levels: elementary, secondary and higher education. Vocational training, adult education, schools or classes for special types of children, and kindergartens also form part of the program in most states.

Parents may choose whether to send their children to their local, free public schools, or to private schools which charge fees. The organization and curricula of private schools and colleges are similar to those of the public schools although

The structure of education in the United States

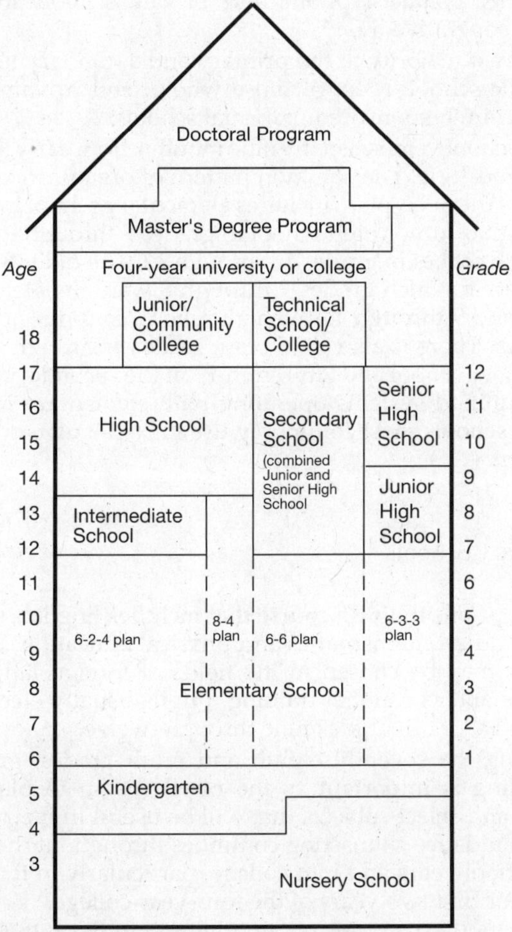

From: *The United States System of Education* (Washington, D.C.: USIA 1984), p. 13.
reprinted in: *American Studies Newsletter* 21, May 1990, p. 11.

the administraton differs. Through the transfer of students and other contacts, public and private schools maintain many cooperative links.

The vast majority at the primary and secondary levels go to public school. Most of those who attend private school attend church-sponsored parochial schools.

The school year is usually nine months, from early September to mid-June. The common pattern of organization, referred to as the 6-3-3 plan, includes elementary school in grades 1 through 6, junior high school in grades 7 through 9 and senior high school in grades 10 through 12. The older 8-4 plan, however, in which grades 1 through 8 were the elementary school and 9 through 12 the high school, continues in many localities. There is also a 6-6 plan, grades 1 through 6 in the elementary school and 7 through 12 in the secondary school. Today unified systems operating both elementary and secondary schools most commonly use the 6-3-3 plan or a 6-2-4 variation. (...)

Secondary Schools

Most pupils follow a course that includes English, science, social studies, mathematics and physical education. Elective subjects may be chosen in the fields of foreign languages, fine arts and vocational training. Pupils usually elect about half their work in grades nine through twelve.

During the seventh, eighth and ninth grades, guidance counseling is important as the pupils begin to plan their careers and select subjects that will be useful in their chosen work. Guidance counseling continues throughout the senior high school years and into college, particularly in the junior college or first two years of the four-year-college.

In general, basic subjects are required in the 10th through 12th years, but in some high schools students may elect an increasing proportion of their work according to their interests.

In addition to these basic subjects – English, science and mathematics, social studies and physical education – larger school systems may offer a selection of courses aimed at three or more levels – academic, vocational and general. The academic program is designed to prepare students for college. Among the subjects added to the core are more advanced mathematics and science courses and foreign languages.

The vocational program may give training in four fields: agricultural education, which prepares the students for farm management and operation; business education, which trains students for the commercial field; home economics, which trains students for home management, child care and care of the sick; and trade and industrial education, which provides training for jobs in mechanical, manufacturing, building, and other trades. This program prepares students either for employment or for further training.

The third program, a general or comprehensive program, combines features of the academic and vocational types. Its introductory courses give an appreciation of the various trades and industrial arts rather than train students for immediate employment or for further vocational education. Those who do not expect to go to college or to enter a trade immediately, but who want the benefits of schooling and a high school diploma, often follow the general course.

Reform

The 1983 study by the National Commission on Excellence in Education (*A Nation at Risk: The Imperative for Educational Reform*) recommended a program of five "New Basics" for the final four years in secondary school.

The minimum course of study for any student seeking a high school diploma would include: four years of English, three years of mathematics, three years of science, three years of social studies, and onehalf year of computer science. For the college bound, the Commission strongly recommended two years of foreign language in high school. These recommendations, and others resulting from similar studies released in the mid-1980s provide the basis for comprehensive changes in the American educational system. (...)

From: *The United States System of Education* (Washington, D.C.: USIA 1984), pp. 10–12. Reprinted in: *American Studies Newsletter (ASN)* 21, May 1990, 10–13

1 ***to comprise*** to consist of; *2* ***vocational*** (berufsbezogen); *8* ***curriculum, -a*** list of topics to be covered in school; *12* ***co-operative link*** exchange of information; *15* ***parochial*** referring to a church district, parish; *30* ***elective subject*** subject chosen voluntarily; *32* ***fine arts*** i.e. art, music, drama; *34* ***guidance counseling*** (Laufbahnberatung); *40* ***basic*** fundamental; *44* ***social studies*** (Gesellschaftslehre); *48* ***core*** basic requirements; *55* ***trade*** here: (Gewerbe); *56* ***manufacturing trade*** industrial production; *61* ***appreciation*** short critical introduction; *62* ***industrial arts*** tasks in the industries; *65* ***benefit*** future support; *69* ***imperative*** urgent necessity; *78* ***to release*** here: to publish; *79* ***comprehensive*** covering all areas

POINTS FOR ANALYSIS AND DISCUSSION

- After reading lines 3–25 of the text, translate the diagram into a talk, in which you tell your group about the prominent features of the structure and organization of education in the US.
- Give a brief outline of the three different programmes offered at American secondary schools.
- What was the result of the study of the U.S. school system published in 1983?
- Point out the similarities and differences between the American and German school system.

- Which of the features of the American school system would you like to be included in our system? Give a speech to your group, in which you give reasons for the changes you advocate.

—— A critical look at the American educational system ——

A Nation At Risk

Our Nation is at risk. Our once unchallenged preeminence in commerce, industry, science, and technological innovation is being overtaken by competitors throughout the world. This report is concerned with only one of the many causes and dimensions of the problem, but it is the one that undergirds American prosperity, security, and civility. We report to the American people that while we can take justifiable pride in what our schools and colleges have historically accomplished and contributed to the United States and the well-being of its people, the educational foundations of our society are presently being eroded by a rising tide of mediocrity that threatens our future as a nation and a people. What was unimaginable a generation ago has begun to occur – others are matching and surpassing our educational attainments.

From: the opening passage of *A Nation at Risk: The Imperative for Educational Reform. Report of the National Commission on Excellence in Education,* Washington, D. C., 1983, 5

1 ***unchallenged*** unrival(l)ed • ***preeminence*** [-'---] superiority; *2* ***commerce*** trading; *3* ***competitor*** [-'---] rival; *5* ***to undergird*** to be the basis of; *6* ***prosperity*** wealth • ***civility*** culture; *7* ***justifiable*** (berechtigt); *8* ***to accomplish*** to reach (an aim); *11* ***eroded*** eaten up; • ***mediocrity*** [--'---] being just average; *13* ***to occur*** to happen; *14* ***to match sth*** to be as good as sth else • ***to surpass sth*** to be superior to sth • ***attainment*** achievement

- What picture of the situation of the American educational system in 1983 do the authors of the study draw?
- Which stylistic means do they employ to emphasize their view?
- Do you think that declining educational standards also threaten German "prosperity, security and civility" (l. 6)? Discuss.

*

U.S. Schools Misuse Time, Study Asserts

Most American students spend only 41 percent of their school days on academic subjects and are taught by harried and overworked teachers who have little time to further their own education, says a study made public today by the National Education Commission on Time and Learning.

The study, a two-year examination of how students spend their days both at school and at home, outlined why American schools lag far behind those in other industrialized countries. It showed that American high school students spend far less time on basic academics than teen-agers in Germany, France and Japan. The balance of American students' time is spent on such things as drivers' education, athletics and non-academic courses.

American students spend about 1460 hours studying subjects like math, science and history during their four years in high school, the report says. By stark contrast, Japanese, French and German students spend 3170, 3280 and 3528 hours, respectively.

Overcrowded Curriculum

The report provides the most specific statistical comparison of study hours yet available, said an official in the Department of Education. It attributes some of the imbalance to comparatively short school days and the nine-month school year, but also criticizes a broad movement to weigh down students' days with subjects outside the traditional curriculum.

"We have been asking the impossible," the report said. "The reform movement of the last decade is destined to founder unless it is harnessed to more time for learning."

The report's results dovetail with those of other studies that have tracked a decline in American students' achievements compared with their foreign peers. But it goes one step further, highlighting the time lost for the social functions schools are expected to perform.

The report noted: "The traditional school day must now fit in a whole set of requirements for what has been called 'the new work of the schools' – education about personal safety, consumer affairs, AIDS, conservation and energy, family life and driver's training."

The result is that secondary school students spend only about three hours a day on core academics.

Applauded by Educators

That point was applauded today by educators who have struggled to raise school standards while trying to meet community and Federal demands for expanded curriculum.

"I think it is pretty radical in terms of the public's perception," said Nancy Kochuk, a spokeswoman for the National Education Association. "As an insider and someone who talks to teachers all the time, there's not that much that is really new. But it is important that parents and others can see that schools are really slaves to time."

Ms. Kochuk said the report, which Education Secretary Richard W. Riley will discuss at a news conference on Thursday, could jog educators to rethink basic things like the standard lenght of class periods. "Kids don't necessarily learn in 42- or 45-minute chunks," she said.

Contrasting American home life with after-school habits in other countries, the report also concludes that foreign students "spend more serious time learning outside the school" and "fritter away less time in front of the television."

The report took note of changing social realities and said, "Family time with children has declined 40 percent since World War II."

Teachers also come under scrutiny, and the report concludes that German and Japanese teachers are given more time for class preparation, grading and their own further education than American teachers, who teach fewer students but have longer hours.

"The commission sensed considerably greater encouragement of teacher professionalism than is apparent in the United States," it said.

Recommendations of the commission were kept general and generic, however, and focused on profound reorganization of the school day around basic learning. The report suggests, among other things, the use of "block scheduling" to allow students to stay with complex material for more than one class period, a greater use of team teaching and increased use of community resources.

The commission also argues against rigid age-based schooling, noting, "It makes no more sense to put a computer literate second grader in 'Introduction to Computers' than it does to place a recent Hispanic immigrant in 'Introductory Spanish'".

From: *The New York Times*, May 5, 1994

to assert [ɜ:] to claim; *2* ***harried*** worn-out; *3* ***to further*** to enlarge; *7* ***to outline*** to explain in short words; *8* ***to lag behind*** to be slower than others; *10* ***academics*** i. e. academic subjects like English, maths etc.; *11* ***balance*** rest; *16* ***by stark contrast*** i. e. by total contrast; *18* ***respectively*** (beziehungsweise); *20* ***specific*** precise; *22* ***to attribute to*** to blame on • ***imbalance*** [-'--] (Unausgewogenheit); *24* ***to weigh down*** to add extra weight to; 27 ***to be destined*** ['destɪnd] to be chosen by fate; 28 ***to founder*** to go down • ***to be harnessed to*** to be tightly connected with; 29 ***to dovetail with*** to fit closely to; 30 ***to track*** to detect • ***decline*** recession; 31 ***peer*** person of the same age, social position etc.; 32 ***to highlight*** (herausheben); 37 ***consumer affairs*** (Verbraucherfragen); 43 ***to raise standards*** (das Niveau anheben) • ***to meet*** here: to fulfil; 44 ***expanded*** more comprehensive; 45 ***in terms of*** with reference to • ***perception*** (Wahrnehmung); 53 ***to jog to*** to turn o's attention to; 55 ***chunk*** (infml) block; 59 ***to fritter away*** to waste; 63 ***to come under scrutiny*** to become the object of research; 69 ***professionalism*** professional competence; 72 ***generic*** unspecific • ***to focus on*** to concentrate on • ***profound*** far-reaching; 77 ***community resources*** (lokale Gegebenheiten); 79 ***rigid*** inflexible

Points for analysis and discussion

- What, according to the text, are the reasons for the decline in American students' attainments?
- What does the commission recommend to improve educational standards at American schools?
- What is your opinion of the commission's recommendations?
- Classify the text-form by mentioning typical features.

*

They're still the ticket to the best colleges: Boarding schools: Pass or fail?

Peter W. Cookson and Caroline Hodges Persell are co-authors of the book *Preparing for Power: America's Elite Boarding Schools.* They discuss their findings in an interview in 1986.

In the opening passage of the article they are quite critical of the atmosphere at prep schools. Then they concentrate on the social function of these schools:

Is it hard for middle-class kids to get into elite prep schools?

Cookson: It's not that hard to get into the average school, but it's difficult to break into the "select 16 schools" like Phillips, Exeter and Groton. There's a prep style that the select schools expect that is hard for a child to acquire unless he or she has the background. Kids are expected to be very self-assured, to verbalize extremely well, to have quite a bit of poise, to look decent. The schools would probably not say that they look for attractiveness, but I think appearance makes a difference.

In addition, kids have to have an intuitive grasp of how to present themselves to questioners so that they can talk about a book or play, giving the interviewer a sense that the child is really tuned in to the cultural world the boarding school feels a part of. After all, these schools were established to create a collective upper-class identity. They have a real mandate to forge kids into what we call in our book "soldiers of their class."

Do the graduates of the select prep schools who go on to top colleges constitute what might be called "the Establishment"?

Cookson: It's at the schools that young people develop networks – what one headmaster has called "resonating relationships" – that last throughout their lives. This provides access at high levels in certain professions, such as law, finance and publishing, especially in firms located in New York and along the East Coast. One study found that 13 elite boarding schools educated 10 percent of the directors of large American business organizations and that 17 percent of those who became directors of two large companies attended one of the

13 boarding schools. Preps also tend to be involved with groups that set much of the cultural agenda for the country.

So, while there are multiple elites in the U.S. – Texas oil millionaires, California computer barons – in certain key areas the prep influence runs quite deep and gives them the quality of an establishment that's quite powerful compared to more-transient power based on economics alone.

(...)

What kind of future do prep schools have?

Cookson: The select 16 schools and other top institutions will always have a group of people supporting them. The lesser-known schools may have a very rough time. During the '70s a number closed. Tuitions have gone up considerably – running up to $ 11 000 annually, with room and board included – and some schools may find it hard to fill their beds. In a society changing as rapidly as ours the value of going away to a prep school may diminish in importance even for those who traditionally used the schools.

(...)

From: *U.S. News & World Report*, Jan 27, 1986, 73f.

14 ***self-assured*** self-confident; *15* ***to verbalize*** to express o.s. • ***to have poise*** (Haltung haben); *19* ***to have an intuitive grasp of sth*** to know sth intuitively; *22* ***to be tuned in to sth*** to fit in well; *24* ***to have a mandate*** to be given a task; *25* ***to forge*** to shape; *31* ***resonating*** (nachhallend); *32* ***to provide access*** to open doors; *40* ***to set an agenda*** to decide what should be discussed; *45* ***transient*** temporary; *50* ***tuition*** fees to be payed to a school or university

Points for analysis and discussion

- What, according to the text, do elite prep schools expect from their students?

- How do prep schools help to keep alive "the Establishment"?
- At the end of the interview Cookson says that in the future "the value of going away to a prep school may diminish in importance". What may be possible reasons for this development?
- Explain Cookson's statement that prep school students become "soldiers of their class" (l. 24).
- What is Cookson's attitude towards prep schools?
- Do you think that prep schools are still in keeping with the times? Explain your view.

A VERY SPECIAL SCHOOL: ST. ANDREW'S

During a Sunday Chapel service on May 13, 1990, Jonathan B. O'Brien, headmaster of St. Andrew's School, says about the 1950s:

"It doesn't surprise me that nostalgia for the '50s has surfaced. Compared to the last three decades, the '50s was an age of innocence. For in spite of laws which prevented people of color from having equal access to the Constitution, in spite of what we call now its sexist attitudes about the role of women in society, and in spite of its hostile reactions to people whose lifestyles and beliefs diverged from the mainstream, I believe the '50s was a "kinder, gentler" decade than any we have experienced since. (...)

We took pride in being stewards of a work ethic which had come to America with its earliest settlers and was responsible for creating products which the rest of the world envied. And if our marriages didn't all last, at least the collective "we" in those days believed in faithfulness and loyalty. And while it might seem quaint and puritanical now, we did not punctuate everyday conversation with obscenities; chain saws were not weapons of choice in the movies we watched; Frank Sinatra's lyrics were about as risqué as things got; and people, by and large, tried to be polite to one another. With all its faults, it was a kinder, gentler time."

From: *St Andrew's Bulletin*, spring 1990, p. 2

6 ***age*** (here: Zeitalter); 9 ***hostile*** opposing; 11 ***mainstream*** general trend; 13 ***steward*** (Verwalter) • ***work ethic*** (Arbeitsethos); 17 ***faithfulness*** fidelity; 18 ***quaint*** strange; 19 ***to punctuate*** to underline; 22 ***risqué*** (gewagt)

Points for analysis and discussion

- What picture of the 1950s does headmaster O'Brien draw?
- What is his main criticism of the following decades?
- By which stylistic devices does the speaker underline his view?
- Do you agree with him? Explain your view.

Some facts about St. Andrew's

In an information brochure of St. Andrew's School we can read:

"Founded by A. Felix DuPont in 1927, St. Andrew's opened for its first session in September 1930 with 35 boarding boys.

In 1973 St. Andrew's became a boarding school for both boys and girls. Today St. Andrew's enrolls 260 students, grades nine through twelve, approximately 45 percent of whom are girls.

All students and faculty reside on campus. St. Andrew's School admits students of any race, color, gender, religious affiliation and national or ethnic origin. Sixty-four percent of our students come from mid-Atlantic states

(New York – Washington, DC), 31 percent come from other states and 5 percent live in foreign countries."

And some more facts:

Tuition, room and board 1995/96: $ 19 300

student-teacher ratio: 7 to 1; average class size: 11 students.

From: *St. Andrew's School: Academic Program 1995–1996*, cover, 1, 3

5 ***to enroll*** to count (as a member); *6* ***approximately*** roughly; *9* ***gender*** [dʒ] sex • ***religious affliliation*** (Religionszugehörigkeit); *10* ***origin*** place/group one comes from; *16* ***ratio*** [ˈreɪʃɪəʊ] (Zahlenverhältnis)

Points for Analysis and Discussion

- Sum up the main facts about St.Andrew's.
- How do the figures compare with your school?

— What St. Andrew's School expects from its graduates —

"We seek to ignite a strong sense of intellectual curiosity and excitement in our graduates and to provide a strong foundation of skills, learning and knowledge that will enable our students to excel in the best colleges and universities in the nation.

We strive throughout our entire program to teach and define high standards of honesty, integrity, compassion and sensitivity that students will carry with them throughout their lives.

We hope to create a boarding school experience that will enable our students to recognize their responsibility for significant service to their community, their nation and their world."

From: *St. Andrew's School*, Middletown, DEL, 1995, 22

1 ***to ignite*** here: to create; 4 ***excel*** to be among the best; 6 ***to strive*** (strove, striven) (nach etwas streben); 7 ***compassion*** sympathy; 12 ***significant*** meaningful • service (Dienst)

POINTS FOR ANALYSIS AND DISCUSSION

- Which are the educational aims at St. Andrew's?
- Which ideas of 'learning' do you see behind such an education?

Residential life

Home Away from Home

It is difficult to exaggerate the importance of residential life at a boarding school. Many of the most valuable lessons our students learn are taught through the interaction they have with their peers and faculty during unscheduled moments on the corridors.

The social structures of corridor life is pyramidal. At the top is the corridor parent. This faculty member has overall responsibility for the students who live under his or her care. If married, the spouse of the corridor parent usually plays an important role. These men and women have chosen careers in a boarding school precisely because they want the kind of close contact with teenagers that such a job offers. They take their in loco parentis roles seriously. Their apartments are open to students, and some may spend as much time listening and counseling as they do teaching or coaching in the more traditional sense. They help their students interpret the occasionally confusing and anxious moments which all teenagers experience.

Next come VI Form students who act as prefects and proctors on all corridors. These students assist the corridor parent in all areas. For example, one is on corridor during study periods to assure quiet. More importantly, they perform the vital function of being an older brother or sister to our younger students. The seniors organize a "Big Brother-Big Sister" pairing with new students, writing them during the summer with tips on what to bring, and then helping them move in and adjust during the first days away from home. Exercising real responsibility and being in a position to help others are among the two most important aspects of a VI Former's education at St. Andrew's. We believe that we are "our brother's keeper," and through the structure of our prefect/proctor system, we try to instill this philosophy in our students.

Finally, the foundation of the pyramid is the form which resides on the corridor. Although they surely learn much of life from their corridor parents and their VI Form prefects and proctors, perhaps they learn most about themselves and others from living with roommates and sharing a "home" with students who have a wide variety of backgrounds and experiences. If they have not learned about compromise, restraint and respect for others before coming to St. Andrew's, they will have ample opportunity to learn. They will find that tolerance, good will and concern for the feelings of others are the touchstones against which their conduct will be measured. They will also have a great deal of fun.

Although we have a few single and triple rooms, most of our students live with one roommate. Our female students live in four different buildings located near Founders' Hall. All our male students live on the second and third floors of Founders' Hall. Most of our corridors have common rooms equipped with television sets and cooking facilities.

From: *St. Andrew's School: Academic Program 1995–1996*, 22f.

4 ***interaction*** exchange of ideas; *8* ***overall responsibility*** i.e. total responsibility; *10* ***spouse*** husband/wife; *14* ***in loco parentis role*** role instead of real parents; *20* ***VI Form student*** student in final two years (mainly in England) • ***prefect*** ['--]

older student responsible for younger ones • ***proctor*** person supervising exams; *23* ***vital*** ['vaɪtl] extremely important; *33* ***to instil(l)*** [-'-] to implant; *40* ***restraint*** self-control; *42* ***ample*** (vielfältig); *43* ***concern*** friendly interest; *44* ***touchstone*** here: criterium • ***conduct*** behaviour

Points for analysis and discussion

- Describe the structure of the school pyramid.
- In which way are students involved in the organization of residential life at St. Andrew's?
- Which duties do the teachers have at that school? In which way does their role differ from that of German teachers?
- Why is the peer group considered important for the development of the students?
- What does this extract from the "Academic Program" of St. Andrew's reveal about the 'spirit' of that school?

*

Community Expectations

Experience tells us that the life and well-being of any community, large or small, rest on the mutual trust, respect and understanding which exist among its members. At St. Andrew's, stealing, lying or any form of dishonesty is simply unacceptable, as is the use or possession of alcohol or other illegal or harmful drugs. There is no visitation in dormitory bedrooms by students of the opposite sex. The School's expectations of a student's personal conduct are high, yet no higher than common sense, maturity and intelligence would dictate.

St. Andrew's operates under an honor code, as well as a code of discipline. An apparent violation of the honor code or of a major school rule would convene the Honor or Discipline Committee, each composed of students and teachers. The committees recommend disciplinary action to the Headmaster when warranted.

Dining and Daily Chores

At St. Andrew's, meals are a time not only for nourishment but also for companionship. Breakfasts are cafeteria-style and informal. Most lunches, and on Wednesday evenings prior to chapel, we gather together for a familystyle meal at which students take turns as waiters. Roughly eight students, mixed by form, sit at tables to dine with faculty and their families. It is a time when we try to slow the pace of our lives and catch up with each other. At the end of such meals, the president of the student body announces items of community interest. Our other evening meals are relaxed, cafeteria-style meals which feature a complete salad and dessert bar. If food is an essential component of our daily lives, so, too, is the time we devote to cleaning up. However, in all honesty, we cannot claim that our students relish this aspect of our routine as much as they do eating. Be that as it may, each student is expected to have his or her room in good shape before classes begin each day. In addition, we are a community which expects all its members to share responsibility for the appearance of our buildings and grounds. Each student cleans a certain area of the School following breakfast. Each job takes no more than fifteen minutes, and all are rotated every three weeks.

From: *St. Andrew's School: Academic Program 1995–1996*, 24

3 ***mutual*** ['mju:tʃʊəl] (gegenseitig); *7* ***visitation*** visit; *10* ***common sense*** (gesunder Menschenverstand) • ***maturity*** physical and mental development; *12* ***honor code*** set rules of accepted behaviour; *13* ***violation*** [vaɪə'leɪʃn] (Verletzung); *14* ***to convene*** to call together; *17* ***warranted*** ['---] officially asked for; *18* ***chores*** routine jobs around the house; *19* ***nourish-***

ment supplying the body with food; *20* ***companionship*** company; *22* ***prior to*** before; *25* ***pace*** speed; *27* ***student body*** all the pupils/students; *29* ***to feature sth*** to have as a main part; *30* ***essential*** very important; *31* ***to devote to*** (widmen); *32* ***to relish*** to enjoy

Points for analysis and discussion

- Which rules are students at St. Andrew's expected to follow?
- How are violations dealt with?
- Which communal duties and responsibilities do students have to carry out?
- Which of the school rules at St. Andrew's do you consider as sensible/too strict? Explain your view.
- What are your impressions of that school after reading the above texts? Which aspects of life at St. Andrew's appeal to you and which do you consider off-putting? Would you like to be a pupil at that school?

WHAT OTHER PEOPLE THINK ABOUT GREAT TEACHERS

"The Best Teacher I Ever Had" by David Owen

The best teacher I ever had in any grade, including college, was Mr. Whitson, who taught sixth grade science. One day, when we were studying electricity, he let us hold hands in a big semicircle while one of us stuck a pencil into an electric arc, so that we could find out what 50 000 volts felt like. (It didn't feel as bad as you would think. The amperage was very low.) (...)

On the first day of sixth grade, Mr. Whitson gave us a lecture about a creature called the cattywampus, an ill-adapted nocturnal animal that was wiped out during the Ice Age. Mr. Whitson passed around a skull as he talked. We all took notes, and later we had a quiz.

When he returned my paper, I was shocked to discover that I had failed. There had to be some mistake, I thought. I had written down exactly what Mr. Whitson had said, yet there was a big red X through each of my answers. Then I realized that everyone in the class had failed. What had happened?

Very simple, Mr. Whitson explained. He had made up all that stuff about the cattywampus. The information in our notes and on our tests was, therefore, incorrect. Did we expect credit for incorrect answers? There had never been any such animal.

Needless to say, we were outraged. What kind of test was this? And what kind of teacher?

We should have figured it out, Mr. Whitson said. After all, at the very moment he had been passing around the cattywampus skull (in truth, a cat's), hadn't he been telling us that no trace of the animal remained? He had described its amazing night vision, the color of its fur and any number of facts he couldn't possibly have known. He had given the animal a ridiculous name, and we still hadn't been suspicious. The zeroes on our papers would be recorded in his grade book, he said. And they were.

Mr. Whitson said he hoped we would learn something from this experience. Teachers and textbooks are not infallible, he said. In fact, no one is. He told us not to let our minds go to sleep, and he told us to speak up if we ever thought that he, or our textbook, was wrong. (...)

In the future, it has been said, everyone will have 15 minutes in which to propose a solution to the crisis in our schools. Mine will be Mr. Whitson. (...) Mr. Whitson gave my classmates and me something very important: the courage to look people right in the eye and tell them they are wrong. He also showed us that you can have fun while doing it.

Not everyone sees the value in this. I once told an elementary school teacher about Mr. Whitson. The teacher was appalled. "He shouldn't have tricked you like that," he said. I looked that teacher right in the eye and told him he was wrong.

From: *LIFE*, Oct. 1990, p. 70

5 ***semicircle*** half circle; *6* ***arc*** (Bogen); *7* ***amperage*** number of amperes; *10* ***ill-adapted*** poorly adapted; *11* ***nocturnal*** nightly; *23* ***credit*** (Anrechnung als Leistungsnachweis); *25* ***outraged*** extremely angry; *31* ***vision*** power of the eyes; *37* ***infallible*** unerring; *42* ***to propose*** to suggest • ***solution*** answer; *49* ***appalled*** shocked

Points for analysis and discussion

- How did Mr. Whitson trick his students?
- What did he want the students to learn?
- Do you think Mr. Whitson was right in his methods? Explain your view.
- What makes a teacher qualify as the best teacher **you** ever had? Give reasons for your answer.

ANOTHER VOICE IN THE CONCERT

Albert Hammond, "The Free Electric Band" (1973)

My father is a doctor,
He's a family man;
My mother works for charity
Whenever she can.
They're both good clean Americans
Who abide by the law.

They both stick up for liberty,
And they both support the law.
My happiness was paid for
When they laid their money down
For summers in a summercamp
And winters in the town.
My future in the system
Was talked about and planned
But I gave it up for music
And a free electric band.

I went to school in handwash shirts
With neatly oiled hair.
The school was big and newly built
And filled with light and air.
And the teachers taught us values
That we had to learn to keep,
And they clipped the ear of any idle
Kid who went to sleep.
Then my father organized for me
A college in the east,
But I went to California,
The sunshine and the beach.
My parents and my lecturers
Could never understand
Why I gave it up for music
And a free electric Band.

They used to sit and speculate
Upon their son's career:
A lawyer or a doctor or a civil engineer!
Just give me bread and water
Put a guitar in my hand
'cause all I need is music
And a free electric band.

My father sent me money
And I spent it very fast
On a girl I met in Berkeley
In our social science class.
Yes, and we learnt about her body
But her mind we didn't know
Until deep-rooted attitudes
And morals began to show.
    She wanted to get married
    Even though she never said,
    And I knew her well enough by now
    To see inside her head.
        She'd settle for suburbia
        And a little patch o' land.
        So I gave her up for music
        And a free electric band.

3 ***charity*** welfare organizations in general; *6* ***to abide by the law*** to keep the law; *7* ***to stick up for sth (stuck, -)*** (infml) to fight for sth; *23* ***to clip*** (infml) to hit shortly • ***idle*** inactive; *35* ***civil engineer*** engineer planning buildings; *52* ***to settle for*** to be satisfied with • ***suburbia*** the suburbs; *53* ***patch*** small area

Points for analysis and discussion

- Which information do we get to know about the parents of the singer?
- What plans did they have for his future?
- Why do they fail?
- What is the singer's protest directed against? What is he searching for?
- Do you think the singer's criticism is justified? Explain your view.

O Robin! My Captain! A powerful teacher is a benevolent contagion, an infectious spirit, an emulable stance toward life by Georg F. Will

Your children have been out of school and underfoot for less than a month and already you are counting the days – minutes, you say? – until school regathers them to its bosom in blessed September. For now, enroll them for two hours in Welton Academy. You, too, might as well matriculate for the pleasure of studying poetry with John Keating.

Keating, played with restrained perfection by Robin Williams (there is no "Goooooooooooooooood Morning Vermont!") is the intense but deft English teacher whose spirit drives "Dead Poets Society". This movie may wean a few adolescents away from addiction to the merely visual. It can spark appreciation of the rapture – that is not too strong a word – they can receive from words. (...)

Hollywood has an almost unconquerable itch for moral black and white, and this movie has a two-hanky ending that manipulates emotions too mechanically. But at the core of the movie is a flinty, unsentimental message: the wildness of life can be dangerously wild. Creativity can have painful costs that must be paid in the coin of personal, family and social stresses.

Speaking of stress, while waiting for September do note that Keating tells the boys they may address him either as Mr. Keating or O Captain! my Captain! (from Whitman's poem about Lincoln's death). This summer, answer your children only when so addressed. It will work wonders for your morale, the tone of your household and the caliber of the long days until Labor Day.

From: *Newsweek*, July 3, 1989, 74

2 ***benevolent*** (gutartig) • ***contagion*** (Ansteckungsherd) • ***an infectious spirit*** a spirit reaching others, too • ***emulable*** worth imitating; *3* ***stance*** attitude; *4* ***underfoot*** (infml) in the way; *6* ***bosom*** ['bʊzəm] (Busen); *8* ***to matriculate*** to enrol; *10* ***restrained*** (zurückhaltend); 12 ***deft*** clever; *13* ***to wean sb away from*** to move sb's interest from; *14* ***adolescent*** youth between childhood and adulthood • ***addiction*** uncontrollable urge • ***merely*** (adv) only, exclusively • ***visual*** optical media; *15* ***to spark*** here: to cause • ***appreciation*** respect • ***rapture*** great pleasure; *17* ***itch*** longing; *20* ***flinty*** cruel; *29* ***morale*** mental strenght; *30* ***Lab(o)ur Day*** USA: 1st Monday in Sept.

POINTS FOR ANALYSIS AND DISCUSSION

- What is the reviewer's opinion about the film? Which reasons does he give to support his view?
- Do you agree with his interpretation of the "message" of the film (cf. ll.17–19)? Give reasons for your view.
- The headline arouses the reader's curiosity. How does the writer succeed in meeting the reader's expectations?
- Analyse the tone which the author adopts in his review. What is the intended effect?

*

The Red, Red Robin Comes Blabbin' Along by John Simon

Let me come out and say it: *Dead Poets Society* (naturally without an apostrophe) is the most dishonest movie I have seen in a long time.

From: *National Review*, September 15, 1989, 54

to blab (schwätzen)

*

Seize the Day? by Harry M. Geduld

(...)

The audience with whom I saw *Dead Poets Society* vociferously applauded Keating as the film's hero. Presumably, their reactions were influenced by Robin Williams's well-established comedic image. However, their response to his character in this particular movie seems to me to be totally misplaced. Keating is a con-artist, not a brilliant teacher, and his students are his misguided victims. He performs stunts that underscore *his* persona instead of teaching literature. He mocks and rejects his class's "assigned text", absurdly prescriptive, but he *himself* never really teaches poetry. In fact, we never see him "analyze" a single poem. He merely *uses* poetry as a springboard for preaching his own romantic "gospel". He announces that the class will read Shakespeare but instead does impersonations: His students get to read only what Keating likes. To hell with the curriculum and to hell with the exams for which he is supposed to be preparing them! One admiring boy tells Keating, "You can go anywhere and do anything". That's fine for the teacher – but what about the students whose school careers his influence so wantonly disrupts?

Ironically, although Keating preaches "all for love", we learn that he has left the girl he loves three thousand miles away in London in order to teach at Welton. For Keating himself, *"Carpe diem!"* evidently means "seize the job!" And, although he preaches individualism, he turns his students into junior Keatings. His students revive *his* old society and use *his* old books and *his* old rituals as a basis for "their" organization. At the end of the film, they can only express "their" rebellious spirit by aping one of his stunts. Most significantly, Neil Perry (Robert Sean Lenard), the student who adopts Keating's philosophy most fervently and most disastrously, is inspired to play Puck in a school production. Shakespeare's mischievous sprite is, of course, an alter ego of Keating.

In the final analysis, Weir's film is about a conscienceless "teacher" who lures his students into fighting his ideological "revolution" for him. He evidently lacks the temerity to try out his ideas on his peers – that is, the faculty. *"Carpe diem!"* says Keating. But the film vividly demonstrates that, for this sort of "inspirational" teacher, the true message is not "seize the day" but, rather, "let those who are most impressionable seize it for you".

From: *The Humanist*, October 1989, 42f.

2 ***vociferously*** (adv) [-'---] noisily; *3* ***presumably*** (adv) possibly; *4* ***well-established*** well-founded; *7* ***misplaced*** out of place • ***con-artist*** (Trickbetrüger); *8* ***stunt*** spectacle; *9* ***to underscore*** to highlight; *10* ***prescriptive*** setting rigid standards; *14* ***gospel*** here: faith; *15* ***impersonation*** imitation of certain persons; *21* ***wantonly*** (adv) recklessly • ***to disrupt*** to tear apart; *27* ***to revive*** to bring back to life; *30* ***to ape*** to imitate unthinkingly; *31* ***to adopt*** to accept for o.s.; *32* ***fervently*** (adv) enthusiastically • ***disastrously*** (adv) fatally; *34* ***mischievous*** planning evil tricks • ***sprite*** forest spirit; *36* ***to lure sb into doing sth*** to trick sb into doing sth; *37* ***temerity*** [-'---] courage

Points for analysis and discussion

- Can you think of any reasons why J. Simon may consider the film as "dishonest"?
- What are H. M. Geduld's main points of criticism?
- By what means does he try to enhance the persuasiveness of his "analysis"?
- Do you share Geduld's negative view of Keating?
- Which of the three critiques comes closest to your own opinion about the film? Do you think that reading the novel has influenced your view?

Copyrights

Walt Whitman: "O Captain! My Captain" / "Poets to Come" / "Starting from Paumanok" / "Song of Myself".
In: Sculley Bradley, Harold W. Blodgett (edd.): Walt Whitman, Leaves of Grass, New York: Norton, 1973, 14, 17f, 28, 89, 337f.

Robert Herrick: "To the Virgins, to Make Much of Time".
In: John Hayward (ed.), The Penguin Book of English Verse, Harmondsworth, 1973, 158f.

William Shakespeare: "Sonnet CXVI".
In: W. J. Craig (ed.), Shakespeare: Complete Works, London: OUP, 1966, 1122.

William Ernest Henley: "Invictus".
In: William Butler Yeats (ed.), Oxford Book of English Verse, Oxford: Clarendon, 1970, 25.

Robert Frost: "The Road Not Taken".
In: Gerald Dewitt Sanders et al. (edd.), Chief Modern Poets of England and America, New York: Macmillan, 1963, II–84.

The United States System of Education.
Washington, D. C.: USIA, 1984, 10–13.

A Nation at Risk.
The Imperative for Educational Reform. Report of the National Commission on Excellence in Education. Washington, D. C., 1983, 5.

U.S. Schools Misuse Time, Study Asserts.
The New York Times, May 5, 1994. Copyright © 1994 by The New York Times Company.

They're still the ticket to the best colleges: Boarding Schools – Pass or Fail?
© U.S. News & World Report, Jan 27, 1986, 73f.

A Very Special School: St. Andrews.
St. Andrew's Bulletin. Middletown, Del., spring 1990, 2.
St. Andrew's School: Academic Program 1995–1996. Middletown, Del., 1995, cover, 1, 3, 22ff.
© St. Andrew's School. Middletown, Del., 1995, 22.

David Owen: The Best Teacher I Ever Had.
© LIFE, Oct 1999, 70.

Albert Hammond: The Free Electric Band.
© IMP, International Music Publications, London.

George F. Will: O Robin! My Captain! A powerful teacher is a benevolent contagion, an infectious spirit, an emulable stance toward life.
© Newsweek, July 3, 1989, 74.

John Simon: The Red, Red Robin Comes Blabbin' Along.
© National Review, Sept 15, 1989, 54.

Harry M. Geduld: Seize the Day?
© The Humanist, Oct 1989, 42f.

Every effort has been made to trace owners of copyright material, but in some cases this has not proved possible and repeated enquiries have remained unanswered. The publishers would be glad to hear from any further copyright owners of texts reproduced in this book.